Two week loan

Please return on or before the last date stamped below.
Charges are made for late return.

19 MAR 1996
CANCELLED

17 MAY 1996
CANCELLED   WITHDRAWN

-3 OCT 1996
CANCELLED

26 OCT 1998
CANCELLED

26 APR 1999
CANCELLED   WITHDRAWN

21 DEC 2001
CANCELLED

TRADE UNIONS
IN WEST GERMANY

TRADE UNIONS IN WEST GERMANY

E.C.M. Cullingford

WILTON HOUSE PUBLICATIONS: LONDON

Published by
Wilton House Publications Ltd
16 Regency Street, London SW1

First Published 1976

Printed and bound in Great Britain
at the Alden Press, Oxford
ISBN 0-904655-09-1

Contents

Foreword

By Heinz Oskar Vetter
President of the German Trade Union Federation (DGB)

It is very seldom that national trade union organisations are described from a foreigner's point of view. Although democratic trade unions are more in the open than most large-scale organisations, not only in their actions and activities but also in their objectives and structure, it is not easy for an outsider to acquire a full appreciation of the detailed functioning of such an organisation as if he were himself a part of it.

That is not the case as regards this book although the question may arise as to what extent the author is to be regarded as a genuine outsider when he was himself present in Germany observing the rebuilding of the movement during those early crucial years.

Comprehensive knowledge and an unconcealed sympathy for the German Trade Union movement (DGB) and its affiliated trade unions are clearly perceptible in this book. That, however, does not prevent the author from seeing and describing us with critical detachment. It is this that gives the book its particular value. It gives the foreign reader the opportunity of forming his own comprehensive picture of the development of German trade unionism over the last thirty years and to learn more of its economic, social and socio-political principles.

The book has also a special value for the German trade unionist. It presents him with a mirror in which he can observe the critical assessment of his organisation by an author who is not himself actively engaged on either side in the conflict of interest between capital and labour.

This book is therefore able to make its contribution towards promoting a better understanding between people and, more particularly, between working people in Great Britain and in the Federal Republic of Germany. The process of increasing integration within Europe is unthinkable without such understanding. Although the trade union movement is essentially international it has always to be borne in mind that the national unions differ from one another in their historic development, ideology, activities and functions. The reason for this is that in their struggle for better standards of living and improved working conditions and in striving for a better economic and social order the trade unions have to react to the circumstances prevailing in their own country. It is thus impermissible for national trade union movements to be played off against one another or for varying attestations to be given as to their economic and social–political 'sense of responsibility'. For example, comparisons are constantly made between the strike propensities of British and German trade unions. In doing so, insufficient account may be taken of the different situations in the two countries to which the TUC and the DGB have to respond; then, too, the differing procedures for regulating industrial conflict may not be taken sufficiently into account. One can well imagine that, given the same conditions as in Great Britain, the German unions might not react very differently from their colleagues there.

Mr. Cullingford's book may help to confirm this observation, more particularly by his detailed description of the German works constitution laws, the system of collective agreements and the functions of the labour courts.

This book can therefore play a part in narrowing the gap in our mutual understanding. It might be well for this publication to be followed not only by a German book about British trade unions but by a similar analysis of other national trade union movements within Europe.

Seen in this way, the book does more than provide information about German trade unionism; it makes a contribution towards the European integration of the trade unions.

Acknowledgement

This account of German trade Unionism since the War owes its origin to a suggestion from the Anglo-German Foundation for the Study of Industrial Society. I should like to express my thanks to the Foundation for its help and encouragement.

There will still be many trade unionists in Germany who have lively recollections of the part played by Mr. Frank Kenny in the years immediately following the 1939–45 War. Himself a life-long trade unionist he did more than anyone during that critical period to help clear the way for German trade unionists to build up their movement anew. He was always at pains – and rightly – to give the credit to the Germans themselves for this achievement but it is fortunate that someone was available at the right time with unique qualifications to smooth the way, obviate misunderstandings and engender ever-growing trust and confidence. It is only appropriate to make this tribute to his memory.

E.C.M.C.

1

The Background: a brief historical sketch

A brief account of the origins of German Trade Unionism seems desirable before attempting to outline the way the movement has developed over the last thirty years. In the Middle Ages brotherhoods of journeymen (*Handwerksgesellen*) had acquired strength and self-confidence and had attained a surprising degree of organisation; records still available of their negotiations with the masters display similarities with modern methods of collective bargaining and interesting methods of arbitration and conciliation were evidently being put to good use.

It was not, however, until the rapid growth of the industrial centres associated with the Industrial Revolution that something like a trade union movement, as we know it, began to emerge. As early as 1848 an All-German Workers' Congress (*Allgemeiner Deutscher Arbeitskongress*) took place in Berlin at which an attempt was made to establish a central 'Workers' Brotherhood' (*Arbeiterverbrüderung*) which, had it succeeded, would have been very much like a central trade union organisation. The next forty years, however, were full of vicissitudes and setbacks and it was not until the repeal of the Socialist Act (*Sozialistengesetz*) shortly after the Ruhr Miners' strike of 1889 that the movement began to emerge in the form it retained until 1932; organisational divisions gradually crystallised during these thirty years that were ultimately to prove fatal in the last critical years of the Weimar Republic. Only if these divisions are kept in mind can an adequate appraisal be made of the remarkable developments that took place in 1945 and the years immediately following – developments that led to the creation of one of the most powerful, influential, wealthy and best organised trade union movements in the Western World.

The trade union organisations

By far the most important of the three trade union organisations that took shape in the eighteen-nineties was the *General-Kommission der Gewerkschaften* known, from 1919 onwards, as the *Allgemeiner Deutscher Gewerkschaftsbund* (ADGB) – the General Federation of German Trade Unions. This owed its being mainly to Karl Legien. Under his leadership there began a series of vigorous campaigns for higher wages and shorter working hours that eventually obliged employers to form a counter-association of their own. Shortly before the first World War the 'Free Trade Unions' (*Freie Gewerkschaften*) federated to the ADGB had already attained a membership of over two and a half millions. They had accumulated considerable sums of money, had set up impressive offices in all the major towns and were running a multiplicity of welfare activities; well edited journals, news sheets and other forms of trade union literature were pouring forth from their printing presses.

In competition with the ADGB were two other important trade union movements. One of these was the Federation of Christian Trade Unions (*Gesamtverband Christlicher Gewerkschaften*). The way for this had been paved by the Catholic clergy under Bishop Ketteler but it was not until the issue of the papal encyclical *Rerum Novarum* in 1891 that Christian trade unions came into being, the Christian Mine Workers' Union (*Christlicher Bergarbeiterverband*) in the van; in 1899 the first Christian Trade Union Congress took place at Mainz. Membership of the Christian trade unions was open to both Catholics and Protestants but, in practice, Catholics predominated. The movement would never have been able to recruit so many members had it not been for the marked anti-clerical and, at times, extreme Marxist attitude of some of the unions federated to the ADGB – an attitude that was to change markedly in the period after 1945, to the considerable benefit of German trade unionism.

Other union activity

But yet another trade union group was active. Though less important than the other two, it was particularly attractive to clerical workers who outnumbered the manual worker members within it by about two to one. It was known as the Hirsch–Duncker movement (*Hirsch–Dunckerschen Gewerkschaften*) after the name of its founders. Max Hirsch had been a devoted student of British trade unionism but some of his movement's earlier characteristics, such as the disavowal of strikes as a bargaining weapon, were to be later rejected although hostility to the Social-Democratic Party remained consistent. This attitude was due to the ADGB's atheistical and Marxist attitude, already mentioned, which alienated many workers who were otherwise not particularly sympathetic to the Catholicism of the Christian trade unions.

A large section of the German trade union movement was in fact inspired at the outset by political leaders who stood far to the left. Under Bebel and Liebknecht, many unions were affiliated to the Marxist First International and, even after the amalgamation of the *Sozial-Demokratische Arbeiterpartei* with Lassalle's *Allgemeiner Deutscher Arbeiterverein*, the 'Free Trade Unions' theoretically continued to accept the Marxist doctrine of the class struggle and regarded the Social Revolution as the ultimate goal. In actual practice the ADGB was a good deal more moderate than the political extremists within its ranks and it displayed no reluctance to negotiate with employers in order to secure improved wages, reduced working hours and better working conditions.

Government attitude during first World War

During the first World War the attitude of the German Government to trade unionism underwent a radical change. At the beginning of hostilities a sort of truce was concluded with the unions and they found that they were being accepted as a necessary, if not wholly desirable, institution. They also found in the military authorities an unexpected ally, prepared often to back them when employers were reluctant to grant concessions. As the war went on it was increasingly taken for granted that the unions had a role to play as spokesmen for the working classes, and, as such, they began to be consulted as a matter of course on food rationing and similar matters. The war had hardly ended – to be precise, it was on 15th November 1918 – when the central organisations of the three trade union movements and the employers' associations drew up an agreement providing for the establishment of a Central Joint Committee (*Zentralarbeitsgemeinschaft*) of trade unionists and employers. Thus by the end of the war the unions were in a much stronger position than at its beginning and clauses aiming at their protection were actually worked into the constitution of the Weimar Republic. In this they were given the freedom to form associations for the maintenance and promotion of satisfactory economic and working conditions. Provision was also made for the setting up of workers' councils and economic councils (*Arbeiter-und Wirtschaftsräte*). These were put into effect by the Works Councils Act of 1920 (*Betriebsrätegesetz*).

The post-war and pre-1939 situation

The future of German trade unionism looked promising. By 1922 there were 49 trade unions with a membership amounting to eight millions. But there was still very little co-operation between the three groups and rifts could be detected within the ADGB itself. Left-wing opinion was impatient of what it regarded as collaboration with the capitalist state and this led the moderates to set out their view with noteworthy clarity in the following statement issued in 1929:

'The State of today is no longer the anti-union State of pre-war times. The unions co-operate with the State and have a far-reaching influence on its institutions, which they can remould and to a considerable extent actually have remoulded.'

The economic collapse that year, however, provided political extremists with just the opportunity they had been hoping for. Faced externally with ever increasing National-Socialist hostility, the German trade union movement was under insidious attack from within by growing Communist activity. This had been going on for some time by skilful eroding tactics but it did not always work in this subtle way and came well into the open when impatient left-wing extremists formed the 'Revolutionary Trade Union Opposition' (*Revolutionäre Gewerkschafts Opposition* or RGO). This, with its notorious network of cells in the main industrial undertakings, played directly into the hands of the right-wing extremists, the National Socialists, who now established as a counter to the 'Revolutionary Trade Union Opposition' their own 'National Socialist Works Organisation'–(*Nationalsozialistische Betriebsorganisation*). At long last the three major trade union groups realised that it was essential for them to co-operate more closely, but it was too late; the ADGB, in particular, had been fatally weakened internally by Marxist activity (as was brought out in the TUC's report, issued shortly after the German unions' collapse, on 'Dictatorship and the Trade Union Movement' which clearly showed how Communist attacks on the unions and the Social Democrats had weakened the whole German labour movement).

Thus, when the Nazis came into power in 1933, the trade union movement was in no position to put up an effective resistance; indeed, it even failed to perceive the nature of National Socialism and to grasp that it was quite as incompatible with genuine trade unionism as was Communism. When the National Socialists declared 1st May a national holiday the ADGB warmly welcomed the measure. Twenty-four hours later all offices belonging to the Free Trade Unions were occupied by the SS and SA, many of their leaders were arrested or in flight and their funds were confiscated. The Christian Trade Union and Hirsch-Duncker movements lingered on for only another month before being dissolved in their turn. What had once been one of the most flourishing trade union movements in Western Europe had apparently been obliterated almost overnight. Trade unionists, not far short of six millions of them, organised by now in 200 unions, woke up to find themselves incorporated in a new organisation, the *Deutsche Arbeitsfront* (DAF). A year later the DAF was made into an affiliated organisation of the NSDAP and became the instrument used by the Nazi Party for carrying out its labour policy – a rôle which today is almost exactly paralleled by the Communist *Freier Deutscher Gewerkschaftsbund* (FDGB) in the German Democratic Republic (DDR).

2

The re-creation of the Movement after 1945

Fortunately, many able trade unionists survived the Hitler regime. Some emigrated and others remained in hiding in Germany. For twelve years they had the opportunity of examining the weaknesses of their movement and of working out elaborate plans for re-creating it as soon as National Socialism was overthrown.

In Britain a number of German trade union émigrés were active and ultimately formed a 'Trade Union Centre for German Workers in Great Britain' under the chairmanship of Hans Gottfurcht. This organisation published in London in the Spring of 1945 'Draft Proposals for the New German Trade Union Movement'. Among the signatories were: Walter Auerbach (later to become Secretary of State in the Federal Ministry of Labour in Bonn) and Ludwig Rosenberg who, during the war years, was in charge of a section in the British Ministry of Labour in London dealing with German and Austrian Manpower. He was later to become President of the German Trade Union Federation (*Deutscher Gewerkschaftsbund* or DGB) from 1962–9.

Underground work during the Hitler regime

Working underground in Germany at the same time were trade unionists of exceptional ability with ample opportunity to analyse the reasons for the collapse of their movement and to work out detailed plans for re-creating it on new and more stable foundations. Most prominent among them was Hans Böckler, the man who more than any other was the creator of post-war German trade unionism. In 1927 he had been elected to the post of President of the Rhineland–Westphalia District of the ADGB and the following year he became a Social-Democrat Member of Parliament. As such he was one of the first members of the Reichstag to be taken into 'protective custody'. Immediately after the capitulation in 1945 he came into contact with British Military Government and set about doing everything in his power to revive trade union activity. Fortunately in the Manpower Division of British Military Government were those well acquainted with his impeccable record and outstanding abilities; this goes a long way to explain why trade unionism was built up more quickly in the British than in the American and French Zones of Occupation. Although in American Military Government's first instructions, issued as early as 28th April 1945, provision was made for the restoration of trade unions, both the American and French commanders refused to permit any kind of zonal organisation. Trade union organisations, divided into trade sections, were permitted but only on a 'Land' or State basis. This insistence by the American and French authorities on decentralisation and federalisation did much to hamper the build-up of trade unionism in Southern Germany in the first three years of the Occupation.

The unions and military government

In the British zone, too, there were initial delays due to what Böckler regarded as unnecessary and over-cautious checks on the speed with which the unions could be re-organised. A promulgation from Military Government issued in August 1945 concerning the formation of trade unions, after emphasising the need for the German people themselves to decide on the form trade unions should take, went on to stress that any such plans would receive the most attentive scrutiny of Military Government. This was followed up in April 1946 by the issue, by Industrial Relations Branch of the Manpower Division, of a very important instruction (Industrial Relations Directive No. 16) which laid down in great detail three distinct phases of trade union development. Böckler chafed at the restraints this Directive placed upon trade union plans, in particular its elaborate provisions for the completion of detailed questionnaires or 'Fragebogen'. But, in practice, Manpower Division wisely chose to turn a blind eye to much that was going on and matters started moving ahead with astonishing speed, leaving the American and French zones far behind. This was because Böckler and his colleagues were already inspiring such confidence in their integrity that Manpower Division officials saw that they could safely allow many activities to develop at a much faster pace than the hum-drum plodding the Directive had visualised. The break-through had, in fact, already taken place a few weeks earlier in Hannover. In advance of a final decision about the Zonal trade union organisation, German trade unionists had reached agreement between themselves on the creation of a Zonal Secretariat. Two of the German émigrés from the 'Trade Union Centre for German Workers' in London came along, bringing with them the greetings of the TUC and the International Transport Workers' Federation – a first sign that German workers might soon be able once more to take up their old international contacts. The men appointed to the Provisional Zonal Executive (*vorläufige Zonenvorstand*) were those mainly responsible – with men like Hans Gottfurcht giving wise counsel in the background – for the new German trade union movement. Their names are worth recording: Hans Böckler, Hans Böhm, Wilhelm Dörr, Hans Jahn, Albin Karl and Franz Spliedt. In addition to the Executive, a Zonal Advisory Committee was set up and among its members were several who were to play a prominent part during the next few years, namely Hans vom Hoff, Anton Storch, Adolf Kummernuss, August Schmidt, Walter Freytag and Frau Liesl Kipp-Kaule (who did so much to call a vigorous organisation for women into being).

It had become evident that matters could be allowed to proceed still more quickly – at a pace never envisaged when Industrial Relations Directive No. 16 was promulgated. The decisive turning point came with the holding of a first fully-fledged Zonal Trade Union Congress (for that is what in effect it was) at Bielefeld from 21st to 23rd August 1946. Bielefeld had been deliberately chosen in view of its close proximity to Manpower Division Headquarters at Lemgo. 375 Delegates were present who could claim to represent well over a million members. The Provisional Zonal Executive and the Provisional Advisory Committee now obtained their formal confirmation and the final authoritative approval of British Military Government was about to be given. At a meeting of the Zonal Executive and the Zonal Committee on 4th October 1946 the Chief of the Manpower Division, Mr. R. W. Luce, was present. He announced, in the course of his long address, that one of his reasons for attending was to demonstrate his willingness to allow Böckler and his colleagues to go ahead with their plans to build up trade unions on an industry basis and, in general, to make it clear that the unions could now proceed with their re-organisation without any further direct intervention on the part of Military Government. This did not mean, by the way, that there was from now on to be any weakening in the friendly collaboration between Manpower Division and the Unions. This remained as close as ever, largely owing to the esteem with which one of Mr. Luce's staff (Mr. Frank Kenny) was regarded by Böckler and his colleagues – with many of whom he was in fact on terms of the closest personal friendship. Leading German trade unionists also sometimes had the opportunity of an occasional talk with British Ministers responsible for German affairs, notably Mr. Hynd and Lord Pakenham.

Assistance from the TUC

It may be recalled that this was the time when Walter Citrine left the TUC to join the Coal Board, later to become Chairman of the Electricity Authority. His place was taken by Vincent Tewson, firmly backed by Arthur Deakin, General Secretary of the TGWU, Sir William Lawther, President of the Miners, Tom Williamson, General Secretary of the GMWU, and Lincoln Evans, General Secretary of the Iron and Steel Trades Confederation. From time to time members of the TUC visited Germany to watch the progress being made by German trade unionism and to give advice as needed. The views they expressed, together with those of people like Hans Gottfurcht, helped to induce Böckler to desist from an unfortunate plan for creating one unified and all-embracing Union, with separate sections dealing with each of the major industries. Once Böckler had allowed himself to be dissuaded from this somewhat Utopian plan, he was free to concentrate all his energies on building up the sixteen Industrial Unions. Unfortunately, he was not to be diverted, however, from an over-insistence on the principle of industrial trade unionism – an attitude that was in the end to lead inexorably to a breakaway on the part of the White Collar Workers' Union, the *Deutsche Angestellten-Gewerkschaft* (DAG).

The name of Wilhelm Dörr has already been mentioned as one of the original six members of the Zonal Executive. From the outset he was responsible for organising white collar workers and it was not long before he began to find himself in conflict with Böckler on the principle of industrial unionism. The dispute culminated in June 1948 in a Special Congress of the Trade Unions in the British Zone, the Recklinghausen Congress. This adopted a resolution providing for a *Berufskatalog* or List of Occupations, the effect of which would have been to limit the White-Collar Workers' Union's organisational scope to Commerce, Banks and Insurance, thus depriving it of about two-thirds of its existing membership and committing it to the unconditional acceptance of the principle of industrial unionism. Dörr and his colleagues declined to accept the Congress's ruling, Böckler proved obdurate and the DAG was expelled from the Trade Union Federation. Corresponding organisations in the American and French Zones, which had by now followed the lead of the British Zone in forming Zonal Federations, came into line with the DAG. To this day the DAG has remained outside the German Trade Union Federation, the *Deutscher Gewerkschaftsbund* (DGB).

The Congress of 1949

Meanwhile repeated unsuccessful attempts to find some basis for collaboration with the trade union movement in the Soviet Zone of Occupation (the so-called *Freier Deutscher Gewerkschaftsbund* or German Confederation of Free Trade Unions) had finally broken down and the way was clear to call a Congress at which all the unions in the Federal Republic (apart from the DAG) were represented. This took place in Munich in October 1949. The British unions were represented by Hans Gottfurcht and by Mr. Robert Willis and Mr. Claude Bartlett, both of whom had previously visited Germany to make contact with the German unions. From the United States of America the AFL and CIO each sent a representative, and the Norwegian, Swedish, Danish, Dutch, Belgian, French, Swiss, Italian, and Austrian movements were all represented – a clear proof of the status which the DGB was already enjoying at this comparatively early date.

It is difficult to recall any one single event in trade union history that achieved so spectacular a success and had such lasting results as the Munich Congress (*Gründungskongress*) of 1949. Perhaps the extent of its achievement can best be assessed by bearing in mind that the description of the organisation of the DGB set out in the next chapter is, in effect, little more than a summary of what was agreed upon and laid down with such conspicuous clarity at the Munich Congress. It was a personal triumph for Böckler and those of his colleagues who had collaborated with him in laying the foundations and erecting the framework of a movement that was to play so noteworthy a part in safeguarding the rights and improving the lot of the workers while simultaneously ensuring national economic prosperity.

3

The present organisation and functions of the German Trade Union Federation (DGB)

The DGB's sixteen affiliated unions (listed in Appendix I) have a total membership of well over seven millions; 5,310,435 are wage earners, 1,381,774 salaried staff and 672,703 civil servants (Beamte). Up to the time of the suppression of the German trade union movement in 1933 there were well over 200 trade unions; many of them were insignificant, however, and industrial unions were even then gaining ground over the older craft unions.

Böckler's achievement in forming a Confederation comprising a limited number of powerful and influential unions covering all workers within various industries, irrespective of occupation, had been somewhat marred by the unfortunate exclusion of the *Deutsche Angestellten-Gewerkschaft* (DAG) or Union of Salaried Staffs (with a membership of some 475,000) owing to its inability to accept the inflexible application of the principle of industrial trade unionism. Another group which would almost certainly have remained outside the Federation in any event is the *Deutscher Beamtenbund* (DBB) or Union of Civil Servants and Officials (membership about 700,000); this, despite many disagreements in principle with the DGB, co-operates in practice fairly closely when it comes to the presentation of pay claims. Of other trade union organisations outside the DGB the most important is the *Gewerkschaft der Polizei*, for police officials; the Christian Trade Union movement is quite insignificant and plays no effective rôle.

The organisational structure

The DGB's organisational structure is made up of a Congress (*Bundeskongress*), Federal Executive Committee (*Bundesvorstand*) and Management Executive Committee (*Geschäftsführender Vorstand*). The supreme governing body is the triennial Congress. The Federal Executive Committee consists of nine full-time officials, including the President and two Vice-Presidents, and the heads of the sixteen affiliated unions. Each of the nine permanent officials, including the President himself, is in charge of a specialist department. The advantage of having nine top-ranking DGB officials is that they are able to give the movement an effective central leadership without imposing an intolerable strain on the President himself; each is free to take a broad and far-sighted view without being pre-occupied with the affairs of his own union. As an act of deliberate policy, two of the nine have always been members of the Conservative Party, the CDU. The DGB's total staff, including those of the district and branch offices, amounts to over 2,000 (not including the staffs, sometimes very large, of the individual unions).

The financial position

The DGB is a very wealthy organisation. Its annual income a few years ago, before present inflationary trends developed, was already assessed at well over DM50 million and now stands at DM104 million. This income derives from union funds – on the average, 12% of the contributions each union receives from its members. The wealth of the trade union movement is reflected by its financial and property interests. One of Germany's largest banks, the *Bank für Gemeinwirtschaft* (which has recently been expanding its international activities and opened a London Branch in June 1974), is run jointly by the co-operative societies and the unions, as is the second largest insurance company, the *Alte Volksfürsorge*. The movement's capital assets were assessed at DM1,500,000,000 in November 1969; a recent assessment puts them at DM3 milliards. The unions' building society, *Neue Heimat* has a capital of well over DM500,000,000. Altogether the trade union movement is understood to have financial resources that now total over DM1430 milliards.

The unions' rôle and objectives

As German trade unionism has made its aim to fight for its objectives on equal terms with those opposing it, the DGB maintains an Economic Research Institute (*Wirtschafts und Sozialwissenschaftliches Institut* or *WSI*) with a large staff which includes some of the most noted economists, statisticians and social scientists in the country. It also runs nine educational establishments (*Bundesschulen*) and social academies (*Akademien*) in addition to those of the individual unions.

The following factors are worth taking into account when considering the rôle played by German trade unions in the industrial relations field:

(1) Trade Unions are not immune from legal process or restraint. German trade unionists do not wish that they should be as they are convinced

that, if this were so, irresponsible militant left-wing elements would then be free to act to the detriment of the trade union movement as a whole; developments in this respect in other Western European countries have received the closest attention in Düsseldorf. The unions are strong supporters of the procedure for dealing with industrial offences by means of a system of Labour Courts (instituted in their present form in 1953) on which employers and trade unions are represented; these courts operate independently of the general juridical system and ensure that cases are handled only by those with expert knowledge of labour practice.

(2) The unions are strongly opposed to State interference in the system of collective bargaining. Collective agreements are freely entered into but, once signed, acquire the force of law under the Collective Agreements Laws (*Tarifvertragsgesetze*) of 1949 and 1952. It follows that they are very carefully drawn up by teams of trained negotiators on both sides. Where breaches of such agreement occur damages can be awarded by the Labour Court.

(3) The DGB laid down guiding principles for strike action at its Munich congress in 1949. These have stood the test of time. No strike may be declared until the possibility of further negotiations has been exhausted; a local union may not start a strike without the authority of its national headquarters; the strike may not take place until there has been a secret ballot and a 75% majority must be obtained before the strike can commence. The secret ballot procedure is regarded as essential: it safeguards trade union members against indirect forms of pressure.

(4) The unions, owing to their anxiety to achieve 'paritätische Mitbestimmung' or fifty-fifty trade union participation in management (about which more has to be said in later chapters), do not consider that the present system of works councils goes far enough. They agree, however, that the system has done a great deal to ensure that 'communications' remain intact and that 'run of the mill' grievances are dealt with very promptly. In addition, the two sides have hammered out procedures in every industry to ensure that disputes and disagreements outside the scope of the works councils are resolved fairly and expeditiously. This has gone some way to remove the feeling that 'management' is something hostile and remote, whose every action has to be treated with suspicion.

(5) German trade unionists wish to see their leaders paid in keeping with their responsibilities and supported by adequate full-time staffs. The leadership has proved equal to the burden imposed on it and has been

successful in bringing the great majority of trade unionists to terms with the rapidly changing economic, social and political conditions prevailing today. Trade union officials are trained with great care, are extremely well informed about the economic situation in general and the state of their industry in particular and have demonstrated on innumerable occasions that they are as mindful of the national interest as they are of the wishes of their membership.

(6) The right to strike (or, for that matter, to declare a 'lock-out') is as much an essential safeguard in Western Germany as elsewhere. But it is regarded as the ultimate sanction, never to be used until all else has failed. Both sides negotiate from positions of great strength but regard recourse to industrial warfare as a palpable confession of failure on their part. The conviction is shared by managements and unions alike that markets may be lost, profits and wage packets endangered, if industry is thrown out of gear by industrial warfare. The prevailing attitude of mind can be summed up quite shortly: 'As disputes have to end at the conference table anyway, why not ensure that they are settled there at the outset?'

(7) The unions wish the State to be scrupulously neutral in industrial disputes. It is taken for granted that the State should not, by paying social security benefits to strikers' families, become a party to an industrial dispute; it is the unwavering view that if the State were to take over the traditional functions of a union's strike fund the authority of the union would be gravely weakened. The union's leaders see great dangers in allowing power to pass to the shop floor and are acutely conscious, in view of increasing Marxist activity, of the risks that would thereby be run of smoothing the way for unofficial strikes.

(8) Although the law provides, in general, no immunity for a trade union or its members, and a union that conducts an illegal dispute at once becomes liable to an action for damages, full protection is nevertheless accorded to disputants engaged in an industrial dispute under the terms of the Collective Agreements Laws. This protection is withdrawn if either party fails to conform to the statutory requirements; strikes not approved by the trade union and not carried out in pursuance of a genuine dispute arising at the expiry of a collective agreement are illegal. Those taking part in unofficial strikes are liable to dismissal by their employer, to expulsion by their union and to an exemplary fine from the relevant Labour Court.

(9) 'Restrictive labour practices' do not exist in West Germany; the expression is, indeed, virtually untranslatable. 'Closed shops' are quite clearly contrary to the Federal Republic's 'Basic Law'. Everyone

is free to join or not to join a union as he or she chooses; legal judgements have repeatedly recognised the right of the individual to remain unorganised without being subjected to any form of penalty in consequence. A decision of the Federal Labour Court in November 1967 under which agreements reached by unions with employers' organisations may not make any differentiation between organised and unorganised workers, however, is understandably regarded by the unions as handicapping them in their efforts to extend their membership and constant attempts have been, and are still being, made to get this decision reversed.

4

The attitude and policies of the German Unions in the Industrial Relations Field

Rivalled only perhaps by Austria, Switzerland, and the Scandinavian countries, Western Germany's well-nigh impeccable industrial relations merit careful study – the more so in view of the difficulties other countries have experienced in this field in recent years. If the reasons for Germany's outstanding performance can be satisfactorily analysed it may be possible to assess whether some of the German methods might be taken over or adapted elsewhere.

Significant factors

Some significant factors in the years immediately following the war cannot, even now, be completely discounted. The allied policy of dismantling factories forced German industry to introduce completely new up-to-date machinery and Marshall Aid became available at precisely the right moment. Among the millions of displaced persons and refugees who entered the Federal Republic from eastern Germany were large numbers of highly trained workers, thousands of whom had held leading positions in industry and commerce; it was the influx of an industrial élite. During the 'despair period' of the first four years after the war enormous efforts were made to put German industry back on its feet and in pursuit of this aim management and labour were at one. These factors, although now of diminishing importance, still lie behind the Federal Republic's present prosperity and, even more significantly, they throw light on the attitude still adopted by organised labour to the need for industrial efficiency.

As to the more recent reasons for Germany's success, considerable weight must be attached to the part played by management. The general level, as distinct from the level attained by the best firms in both countries, cannot but be regarded as generally higher than in Britain. Fifty years ago the education of managers in Weimar Germany was already regarded as of paramount importance; universities and Technische Hochschulen were running flourishing management courses even in the twenties. Since the War further strides have been made in the field of management training. Several universities now have well-run departments of *Betriebswirtschaft* in which economics and management training are combined; most Technical Institutes of university status also have departments which hold similar management training courses. Although much attention has been given in recent years in Britain to systems of management training, the fact remains that Germany has a very long lead; inevitably much of Britain's management remains amateur by comparison. The tradition that the German manager is the first to start work every morning has also helped; the workers can never suspect that management may be putting anything less than the maximum of effort and hard work into the undertaking.

Management/Union co-operation

Good management alone would not, of course, account for Germany's industrial and economic successes, even though the doctrine seems relevant that there are no bad soldiers so long as there are enough good officers. The attitude of the German trade unions is enormously significant. Ever since Böckler and his colleagues re-created the movement, the unions have been consistently behind management in attempting to improve the efficiency and competitiveness of industry. Whenever management has sought to increase productivity it has always had the comforting knowledge that it could rely on union support. Export is a German political principle to which both sides of industry subscribe with equal fervour. There is not much, it would seem, in the belief that the average German worker is by nature inclined to work harder or faster than his British counterpart; what is more to the point is that German management sees to it that he works with greater sustained intensity.

Another fact that may be mentioned in passing is the enthusiasm of the unions for improving the already high standards of German vocational training. The German systems used to suffer from the handicap of being somewhat rigid but increasing attention has been given in recent years to ways whereby they can be more rapidly adjusted to changing technological needs. Free of demarcation disputes and inter-union rivalries, it is the unions that have taken the lead in urging that training should be as broadly based as possible so that a man may change both trade and industry as occasion demands.

Perhaps it is unfortunate that Britain did not have the opportunity presented to Germany immediately after the war of constructing a simple pattern of industrial unions – although had it not been for Böckler and his team of very able colleagues it does not follow that the opportunity thus presented would necessarily have been seized. Up till 1933 – when trade unionism was temporarily swept away – Germany presented the familiar picture of a multiplicity of unions (at least 220) some large, some small, some craft, others industrial unions. Much worse than this, as described in the opening chapter, the unions were divided into three main groups – Socialists, Christians, and Liberals. The achievement of the able group of trade union leaders in 1946 and 1947, whole-heartedly backed by the Manpower Division of British Military Government and with the approval of British trade unionists, is the greater because many of the union leaders had to rid themselves of doctrinaire neo-Marxist tenets held in pre-war days with much greater conviction in Germany than in Britain.

By 1949 the post-war German trade union movement was already firmly established and was recognised as one of the soundest democratic elements in the country. It has never shown any disposition to walk backwards into the future. Convinced that the new problems of the technological age must be mastered if the movement is to have its proper place in the modern democratic State it has acted accordingly; reference has again to be made to the foresight of the Trade Union Federation (DGB) and the larger unions in establishing their own well-paid teams of economic and financial experts able to hold their own in disputes on economic matters both with the employers and, if need be, with the government.

Responsibilities in social, economic and cultural policies

For the discharge of its responsibilities in the fields of social, economic and cultural policy the DGB employs a large staff at its extremely modern and palatial headquarters in Düsseldorf. Its Executive Committee consists of the President and eight whole-time members completely free of the distractions of simultaneously having to run the affairs of a union. Although it has no direct control over the wage negotiations with employers of its constituent unions, the Federation's influence counts for a good deal behind the scenes and it has always been on the side of moderation. Notwithstanding the autonomy of the individual unions, the Federation's triennial Congresses make pronouncements on general policy and on wages and allied matters (above all, on such matters as *Mitbestimmung*); the DGB's aims were clearly proclaimed in November 1963 when a new 'Basic Programme' was formulated and the lines then laid down were broadly followed until re-drawn in a further 'Programme of Action' agreed in Berlin in 1972.

Union Membership fees are appreciably higher than in Britain, being in theory the equivalent of one hour's earnings in the week, or 2% of the monthly salary. If the principle is not very strictly honoured in the observance – and considerable variations do in fact exist between the membership fees of the various trade unions – union fees are nevertheless high by any standards. The Trade Union Federation gets 12% of the contributions received by each union – and the sixteen constituent unions collected contributions a year or two ago that were reckoned to amount to DM865 millions. Reference has been made elsewhere to the way in which the enormous wealth of the German trade union movement is reflected by its financial and property interests.

With this wealth behind them, the Trade Union Federation and its affiliated unions are in a position to let it be known to the employers, on the rare occasions when a strike becomes a possibility, that they have the financial resources to make it a long one. But a strike may only take place after various motions have been gone through in accordance with guiding principles laid down by the Federation at its Munich congress in 1949. As has already been mentioned, no strike may be declared until the possibility of further negotiations has been exhausted; a local union may not start a strike without the authority of its national headquarters and a strike may not take place until there has been a secret ballot of all union members of more than three months' standing and a 75% majority is needed before a strike can commence. If a strike occurs which has not been properly authorised it is the union's responsibility to ensure that work is resumed immediately. Unofficial or 'wild-cat strikes' are therefore very rare apart, of course, from such incidents as a short protest stoppage if, to take a typical example, workers are incensed by some high-handed action on the part of a foreman. Public opinion and trade union opinion are at one in holding that those who flout solemn undertakings entered into between the two sides and who choose to ignore the opportunities provided for redress (including those provided by the works councils) should be brought to book.

If a wild-cat strike takes place the workers concerned can be brought before a Labour Court and, if it were conclusively proved that they had flouted a properly negotiated agreement containing rules for dealing with grievances, they would receive exemplary fines. Trade Union opinion has almost invariably been on the side of the local Labour Court as the impartiality of these courts has become generally accepted. The German system of labour jurisdiction in the form in which it now operates goes back to 1953, deriving from the *Arbeitsgerichtsgesetz* of September that year.

It operates independently of the general system of jurisdiction, there being a Federal Labour Court as supreme instance, twelve 'Land' (or State) Labour Courts and 113 local Labour Courts. Generally speaking, the Labour Courts have a chairman and two lay members or assessors representing workers and employers respectively. The chairman is required to have special knowledge and experience in the field of labour law and labour practice. The assessors are selected from a list of nominations drawn up by trade unions and by employers' associations and are appointed for a term of four years. The fees are much lower than in the Civil Courts and frequently do not have to be paid at all. Those found guilty are appropriately fined – the mistake of providing 'glorious martyrs' by sending them to prison has been studiously avoided.

Owing to the elaborate procedure for the conduct of industrial disputes it follows that there is always adequate notice when a strike is pending. In practice, as a secret ballot has first to be organised to secure the requisite 75% majority, employers can reckon with not less than two weeks' notice. Vitally important from the point of view of industrial efficiency is, too, the knowledge the employers have that a strike can be effectively ruled out so long as a collective agreement is current; delivery dates can accordingly be quoted with complete confidence.

The part played by legislation

The part played by basic German legislation in this happy state of affairs is extremely significant. It is regarded as proper and, indeed, essential by the unions themselves – the more so as it does not continually obtrude itself. The 'Collective Agreements Laws' (*Tarifvertragsgesetze*) recognise the unions for negotiating purposes; collective agreements – freely entered into – are enforceable at law under this Act. They are enforceable only between the parties themselves, i.e. the trade union and the employers' association that were the signatories, although the Federal Ministry of Labour may, if a special committee so recommends, make a 'declaration' as a result of which the terms of the collective agreement may have to be observed throughout the industry concerned. Actions for the enforcement of collective agreements are brought before Labour Courts, at District, 'Land' or Federal level. The Labour Court can award damages in actions for breach of collective agreements, and these can amount to the full loss suffered by an employer as a result of a strike in breach of an agreement.

Although the Collective Agreements Laws are always there in the background, there has been a marked tendency for the two sides to draw up their own rules for avoiding disputes. They take pride in putting their house in order without outside interference. Arbitration is a purely voluntary matter but most collective agreements contain provisions on conciliation which put into effect the terms of a Model Conciliation Agreement negotiated between the Trade Union Federation and the employers in 1954. A procedure for conciliation by a joint 'Conciliation Office' is laid down and if the Office fails to bring the parties together it may make recommendations. These do not have to be accepted but, if accepted, they then have the force of a collective agreement. No coercive action is allowed until the conciliation procedure has failed. Of particular significance is a far-reaching conciliation agreement signed in May 1964 by the Engineering Employers' Association and the Metal Workers' Union. The conclusion of this agreement indicated that what was once Germany's most left-wing and militant union had at last ranged itself solidly alongside the employers in asserting, in effect, that they shared the belief that industrial strife – formerly more or less a commonplace – has in the post-war world become too harmful to be indulged in by a major industrial nation anxious to attain and maintain higher standards of living while avoiding the risks of high inflation.

Fundamental attitudes to industry's competitive capacity

This fundamental attitude of organised German labour to the need for preserving and developing industry's competitive capacity at all costs may well be due not only to the post-war 'despair period' but to the memories of working-class sufferings during inflationary periods – to the German worker unemployment is bad enough but galloping inflation is far worse. He is haunted by the fear that markets may be lost if his industry is thrown even momentarily out of gear. Here again the works councils and economic committees ('*Wirtschaftsausschüsse*'), set up by the original Works Constitution Law and amplified by the later laws of 1971 and 1976 – of which more will be said in a later chapter – play their part in ensuring that German workers are made acquainted with the economic facts of life.

Incidentally, as an indication of the German trade union movement's sense of responsibility, any union which plans a strike in such essential services as food production, power, gas or water supply, sewerage, public health, transport and coal mining, is compelled to notify the Federation's Executive Committee in good time of its plans for action, with details of the emergency measures contemplated to ensure that essential services are maintained. If a strike takes place which fails to conform to the guiding principles mentioned above no benefits are payable, but, in cases where in the interests of the general trade union movement it is deemed necessary, the Federation's General Council may grant financial aid and call on other unions to contribute. As already mentioned, a legal strike can only take place on the expiry of a current collective agreement; during the currency of an agreement the parties may not resort to coercive action in any matter which is regulated by the agreement. Even if they were tempted to do so, the risk of an action in the Labour Court and the consequent award of heavy damages would be a deterrent. The law provides, in general, no immunity for a trade union or its members although, on the other hand, the fullest protection is accorded to disputants who are engaged in an industrial dispute under the terms of the Collective Agreements Laws.

The works councils

Reference has repeatedly to be made to the works councils. This is the place to emphasise the opportunities these councils provide for getting abuses quickly righted and the part they play in fostering good relations between management and men. Although, having regard to the present climate of opinion and the differences in company law, the fundamental British objection to the Co-determination Law of 1951 (applying fifty-fifty co-partnership in the coal and steel industries) seems hardly likely to be shaken, i.e., that it is management's job to manage and that workers should not attempt to sit on both sides of the table at once, this objection has no conceivable relevance to the way the works councils operate. It has over the years been proved to be perfectly feasible for works councils to have legal powers to intervene in a very wide range of matters such as the determination of works rules, starting and stopping times, holiday schedules, recruitment, transfers and dismissals, settlement of piece rates, alteration in working methods, etc. The system has, in general, worked out in such a way as to ensure that, throughout German industry, management is kept in close touch with its employees, keeps them informed of its major plans and programmes and has the opportunity of listening to their ideas, wishes and suggestions. Thus, when considering German industrial relations, the system of works councils, particularly in the form that was re-affirmed by the 1971 Law, must be given due weight. It is a sane piece of industrial democracy that ensures that grievances are quickly nipped in the bud.

Apart from all that has been said above, the overwhelming majority of German workers have not forgotten how greatly their lot has improved over the last twenty years; they are reluctant to do anything to imperil this prosperity. The belief is as widespread in Western Germany as it is in the United States that 'in a progressive country change is constant' and the German unions and their teams of back-room boys are, therefore, unflagging in their attempts to assess the outcome of significant trends over the next ten years in order that policies and demands may be adjusted accordingly. Although the full impact of automation in the strictest sense of the word, i.e. the feeding of machines by machines, has still to make itself felt to any large extent in Germany, the unions – more particularly the Metal Workers' Union – are convinced that this type of automation is going to make itself increasingly felt. The unions actually welcome automation and thorough-going rationalisation as they are satisfied that to try and slow down such inevitable processes of development would in the

long run be fatal to the industrial efficiency on which their livelihood
depends. The unions, in attempting to assess the effect of the anticipated
yearly increase in the gross national product, have satisfied themselves
that the trend is going to be in the direction of reducing working hours. As
to how these fewer hours should be worked they have a fairly open mind
and, besides the obvious shortening of the working week, they contemplate
such alternatives as introducing lower ages of retirement or progressively
extending the school-leaving age.

Union responsibility and authority

It is tempting to suggest that there may be two reasons why the German
system of industrial relations works so well. First of all, much of what has
been said above might almost be summed up by saying that, apart from all
the intangibles (a really good spirit within an undertaking is not, of course,
something that can be created in five minutes), industrial relations are
vastly the better when management and men are kept in day-to-day touch
and minor grievances are not allowed to fester (cf. the role of the works
councils). The other thing is that a proper emphasis on trade union
responsibility and the authority of the leadership, coupled with the
authority of the Labour Courts, makes it impossible for irresponsible or
politically motivated persons to flout their union and ride roughshod over
industrial agreements.

5
Strikes in Western Germany in the period up to 1969

The foregoing chapter may be thought by some to present an idealised picture. The reply of German trade unionists to those who criticise them for being insufficiently 'strike-happy' would, however, be to point to what their policies have achieved for their members – that is, a standard of living over the length and breadth of the land that would have been thought unrealisable as recently as fifteen or twenty years ago. And although strikes have been few and far between in post-war Germany the few that have occurred serve to give the lie to those who believe that the German worker is a docile spiritless fellow, too much inclined to truckle to authority. That the German worker is really not much different from his British counterpart is shown by Germany's strike record from 1890 to 1932. In terms of strike statistics it will in fact be found that there was surprisingly little to choose between the militancy of the German and the British worker before 1914 or, indeed, for that matter right up to the thirties. Even after the German trade union movement's basic reconstruction after the War, several strikes occurred during the early fifties, although after 1958 strikes, or even the threat of a strike, became more and more exceptional. Unquestionably, Böckler and his colleagues at the time of the 1949 Munich Congress were anxious to devise procedures that would avoid any repetition of the incessant damaging strikes that had occurred in the past and wished to ensure that the unions could achieve their objectives whenever possible without strike action. Nevertheless, in this imperfect world German trade unionists are well aware that they must have the strike weapon ready to hand even if they do not believe that it will rust if not put to frequent use.

The major industrial disputes

All told, there have been only five industrial disputes of major significance in Western Germany since the War, as follows:

(1) The Metalworkers' strike in Schleswig-Holstein in the winter of 1956–7.

(2) The Metalworkers' strike in Baden-Württemberg in 1963.

(3) The 'Wild Week' of unofficial strikes in September 1969.

(4) The Metalworkers' strike in Baden-Württemberg in 1971.

(5) The Chemical Workers' dispute of 1971.

The two most recent disputes, those that occurred in 1971, present features of such interest as to merit analysis in separate chapters. The present chapter, therefore, deals only with the first three disputes.

The Metalworkers' strike in Schleswig-Holstein is interesting in that it had nothing whatever to do with wages. It seemed serious enough at the time, but it was concerned solely with technical matters of specifically German interest concerning holidays and sick pay. The issue was fought out by the Metal Workers' Union (*Industriegewerkschaft Metall*) within the boundaries of Land Schleswig-Holstein and did not spread to other parts of the Federal Republic. Suffice it to say that the union successfully made its point although its action was called into question in the courts and it was subjected to an enormously heavy fine – a fine which the employers eventually, and very wisely, decided not to force the union to pay, particularly as the point of principle at stake was one with which some of the employers were themselves by no means unsympathetic.

All the other disputes had to do with wages issues and, as such, have much closer similarities with strikes in Britain. But first of all, before dealing with trade union aims and tactics, some description is called for of the way the employers are organised.

Employer organisations

Employers' organisations were abolished, like the trade unions, in 1933 but they were slower than the unions to get started again after the War. It was 1950 before a Confederation of German Employers' Associations, the *Bundesvereinigung der Deutschen Arbeitgeberverbände* (BDA), emerged with its headquarters in Köln. Its first President, Dr. Raymond, had a difficult time in confronting the champions of labour on the one hand and in dealing with his own recalcitrants on the other – employers of the 'old school' were apt to protest against any 'pusillanimous' attempt to meet the unions half-way. Raymond may not have been quite tough enough for his job but he was one of the nicest of men. The unions learned to appreciate his merits and he came to be regarded by most of them with liking and respect. When he was succeeded by Dr. Paulssen, in 1953, the employers were already getting better organised. Raymond's views as to the need for establishing closer contact with the unions were shared by Paulssen but from this time onwards it was clear that wage negotiations were going to become much tougher than they had been during the years when both sides were concentrating in the main on getting their industries going again.

After their initial hesitant start, the employers' organisations began rapidly building up their strength. The ill-disciplined oddly assorted employers' *Verbände* began to close their ranks and to confront the trade union protagonists with well-organised federations and teams of negotiators no longer liable to be put to rout at the first skirmish; from 1956 onwards the mere mention of the word 'strike' ceased to be sufficient to bring employers to terms. Paulssen called for increasing toughness in negotiations although this toughness was, in the Raymond tradition, sometimes accompanied by a certain sweet reasonableness and courtesy of approach seldom, if ever, experienced by trade unions from employers' organisations in pre-war Germany.

In 1964 Professor Balke (a former Minister of Atomic Affairs) succeeded Dr. Paulssen. He was to remain President until 1969 when he was succeeded in turn by Dr. Otto Friedrichs. He found himself leading a better organised and stronger employers' organisation than would at one time have been thought possible. But employers and employers' associations in West Germany do not take any more kindly than their counterparts in other countries to receiving anything in the nature of 'instructions' from the Head Office of their Confederation – 'solidarity' seems to be even more difficult to achieve among employers than it is in the trade union world. Moreover, in some industries employers may either be organised in *Handwerkskammern* or *Industrie und Handelskammern*, roughly according to the size of their undertaking. But particular weight must be given to the strength of their organisations in the more important industries. It is significant that, of the various associations affiliated to the BDA, the Engineering Employers' Federation (*Gesamtmetall*) is exceptionally well organised. As will later be seen, it gave a massive demonstration of strength during the engineering dispute in Baden-Württemberg in 1963. The Chemical Employers' Federation is also strong and well organised; in some industries the employers' organisations are less efficient and in others rather ragged but there are few industries in which the unions do not find themselves confronted by well-knit organisations capable of enforcing reasonably tight discipline on member firms. It is important to add that, in attempting to assess the strength of employers' organisations, it must not be overlooked that they have ultimately the Federation of Industrialists, the *Bundesverband der Deutschen Industrie* (BDI) behind them. The two organisations have never merged as have the equivalent organisations in Britain and, although it now seems possible that Dr. Hanns-Martin Schleyer, who has been President of the BDA since 1973, will early in 1977 take on the office of BDI President as well, there seems to be no intention of merging the two organisations completely: their tasks are always claimed to be too diverse as to make this possible or desirable.

In the period from 1949 to 1962 the relatively modest wage demands of the unions had, as already mentioned, seldom needed pressing very hard; employers put up little more than a token resistance before agreeing to pay a fair proportion of what was being asked. But as 1963 opened with the customary series of wage demands the atmosphere changed: employers' associations began calling on their members to resist. Some kind of confrontation had been expected sooner of later; indeed, it was thought less to be a question of whether there would be a 'show-down' than when, and in what industry, it would occur. In the event, the issue came to a head in April, the chosen battle-ground being the engineering industry in Land Baden-Württemberg. A fortnight's strike and lock-out was involved, bringing in some 900 firms and over 450,000 workers before a compromise settlement was reached which set the pattern for wage increases throughout the rest of industry.

The Metal Workers' strike

The union involved was, as in 1956, the Metal Workers' – the most powerful of the DGB's sixteen unions. With a membership even then approaching 2,200,000 it was not only West Germany's largest union; it was also the largest and most powerful trade union in the free world and probably the best organised. Led by the redoubtable Otto Brenner, it had always been in the van with wage claims and, by reason of its wealth and the efficiency of its organisation, was confident that it would, as usual, get its demands accepted. Unfortunately for the union, however, *Gesamtmetall*, the Engineering Employers' Federation, had in recent months been brought up to a state of high fighting efficiency by its chairman, Herr van Hüllen, and was quite willing to try a throw. Not until the appointment of van Hüllen at the end of 1961 had Otto Brenner had to encounter a protagonist with a determination equal to his own.

In March and April the all too familiar processes associated with an engineering wages claim were gone through to the accompaniment of increasingly hostile noises from both sides. But when, after the usual flourishes, the strike vote was taken (85% were in favour) and the pistol was levelled at the head of the employers, the union leaders suddenly found themselves, to their discomfiture, looking down the barrel of a weapon the employers were pointing at them – the dreaded lock-out. The

lock-out is not a weapon lightly used by any German employers'
association but on this occasion it was the one wholly effective counter-
move to the union's tactics of striking at carefully selected firms in South
Germany where a stoppage would hurt most. The employers, just like the
union, had for twelve months been planning every detail of their campaign
and the uncompromising thoroughness with which the lock-out was put
into operation paid testimony to the effectiveness of their organisation.
Thus, instead of disrupting production at a few key firms employing less
than 100,000 workers, the dispute spread overnight to 900 firms with well
over 450,000 workers. This was bad enough but there was a more serious
risk in the offing – the possibility that the strike might spread to the Ruhr.
Both sides were equally reluctant to face such a development particularly
in view of the hostility and trenchant criticism to which the dispute was
giving rise throughout the community. Before ten days were over they
responded with alacrity to an invitation from the Economics Minister, Dr.
Erhard, to meet him at the conference table. Twelve hours of discussion
resulted in a compromise solution (a 5% wage increase) for which the
Minister was rightly given the highest credit on account of the skill and
tact he had shown in mediation. It was his most popular and successful
action in the last few months before he became Chancellor.

The big strike of 1963 effectively cleared the air. The employers might
in the long run have beaten the union to its knees, but they were aware that
other wealthy unions were getting ready to come to its financial support,
to say nothing of the Trade Union Federation, the DGB. No one wanted
such a large-scale confrontation. Both sides, too, were a little alarmed by
the very success of their militant measures and were wondering how they
would get the genie they had conjured up back into the bottle. Neither van
Hüllen nor Brenner had ever had quite the same enthusiasm for a fight to
the finish as their lieutenants had been showing in Baden-Württemberg.
Brenner had often been criticised for being one of Germany's most radical
union leaders, but in the last resort he showed himself on this, as on other
occasions, to be no 'wild man' and drew back the moment he saw that his
industry was likely to suffer serious damage.

When the dispute was at its height many voices began to draw attention
to the success of the different style of negotiation adopted by more
moderate unions, notably the Construction Workers, and asked why their
example could not have been followed. All this was not lost on the
engineering industry and within twelve months a Conciliation Agreement
was reached between the two sides that helped to keep the peace for
several years.

'The golden age of German trade unionism'

Not only within the engineering industry but throughout industry as a whole a period of excellent industrial relations followed. For the next few years industry was free of the slightest dislocation through strike action. Despite the slight industrial recession (the 'Mini-Recession') of 1966/1967 (during which the unions exercised noteworthy restraint in refraining from pressing wage claims) the lot of trade union members continued to improve from year to year – so much so that some have regarded this period as the 'golden age of German trade unionism'. The year 1968, in particular, among so many other successful years for employers and trade unionists alike, stands out as a peak. Some unions, of course, did better for their members than others, but all were clearly justified in lifting early in the year the self-imposed restraint they had exercised throughout 1967; wage increases averaging overall about 5·8% were thereafter negotiated without imposing a strain on the economy. Indeed, by the Autumn, the Minister of Economics was already urging the unions to press for increases of $6\frac{1}{2}$% in order to augment mass purchasing power and in December the Council of Economic Advisers (*Sachverständigenrat*) that proffers advice to the Government saw fit to point out that wages and salaries were lagging too far behind the justifiable rate of growth. The few little strikes that occasionally took place usually had the aim of clearing up some point of principle, and the number of working days lost during the first ten months of the year totalled only 12,000 (in comparison with the United Kingdom's figure for the same period of 4,193,000). Strike statistics are always suspect and often misleading (particularly as, unlike the German, the British figures exclude all stoppages involving fewer than ten workers or lasting less than one day), but during the course of the year the comment was made that Britain was losing through strikes almost as many working hours on any one day as West Germany in the course of a year. (By 1970 the comparable statistics of working days lost through strikes that year were: West Germany 93,000 days; Britain 10,970,000).

The year 1968 opened, as it happened, with a serious industrial problem: the future of the Ruhr coal-mining industry. Due in no small part, however, to the statesmanship, foresighted action and determined pressure of the Mineworkers' Union (*Industriegewerkschaft Bergbau und Energie*), a satisfactory solution was found in the setting up of the Ruhr Unitary Mining Company, the *Einheitsgesellschaft*. The Construction Workers' Union (about which more is said in a later chapter), true to its traditions, was pressing ahead in close collaboration with employers in the task of modernising the building and civil engineering industries and in trying out still better methods of keeping work going during bad weather. The Metal Workers' Union negotiated a special rationalisation agreement with the employers with a view to stepping up the pace of industrial change with proper regard to the interests of the workers; it also held in March the third of a series of Automation Conferences it had been sponsoring, attended on this occasion by leading experts both from Europe and America. The Chemical Workers' Union, taking a leaf out of the Metal Workers' book, negotiated its own progressive rationalisation agreement. Meanwhile the unions were unitedly urging the need for better vocational training, in particular better adult training and re-training, and the training of trainers. The text book produced by one union on training for automatic data-processing was found so good that it was officially adopted by the Labour Administration. Few unions have the resources to run the vast congresses periodically organised by the Metal Workers' on automation and rationalisation but one union after another followed the lead given by the Textile Workers' and the Construction Workers' Union in announcing their willingness to back employers through thick and thin in speeding up the process of modernisation – provided always that there was adequate prior consultation and that proper measures were worked out to assist those made redundant.

The unofficial strikes of 1969

During the first half of 1969 matters seemed to be going still better. Towards the end of the Summer, unemployment had virtually ceased to exist (just under 0·5%) and spectacular increases in individual productivity and overall production continued unabated. Such problems as existed were mainly those created by unparalleled prosperity. Everything seemed to be going so smoothly that a short and sharp series of strikes that suddenly occurred in September in the Ruhr and Saar took everyone very much by surprise. It was a bolt from the blue and the effect on politicians, employers, trade unions and the general public was profound. The fear was expressed on all hands that the Federal Republic might, at long last, have caught the 'English sickness' – a sickness reported on day by day in the Press and the more dreaded since, in German eyes, it was now reaching epidemic proportions. Wild-cat strikes by small groups of workers had never previously worried anyone in Germany – it was taken for granted that the Labour Courts would take care of them! But the spectacle of the whole labour force of one factory after another coming out spontaneously on unofficial strike was something quite new and thoroughly alarming – it had never been thought possible, for one thing, that the unions could get so much out of touch with their members.

It all started in a way familiar enough in Britain. The management of one of the largest Ruhr steel works, after dealing lackadaisically with a very reasonable claim for an additional 20 Pfennigs an hour, unwisely decided to see whether a small saving might not be effected by offering a mere 15 Pfennigs. A mood of mild resentment turned at once to angry exasperation and the morning shift spontaneously stopped work. With a pusillanimous haste quite uncharacteristic of German management, the firm capitulated and agreed to pay 30 Pfennigs. Work resumed at once but the alacrity with which the purse strings had been loosened had not gone unnoticed and a chain reaction was set off which quickly affected a number of other Ruhr steel works before spreading to the Saar coal mines. In retrospect it seems strange that employers riding the crest of a wave of unparallelled prosperity should have been so blind as not to perceive that workers would hardly regard an increase of 2% in their wages as bearing any adequate relation to soaring increases in profits of 20% or more. The German worker likes to see his firm making bigger and better profits but he does expect a proper share of those profits to come his way.

Particularly surprising was the way in which the Metal Workers' Union was, for once, caught napping. Ironically enough, the union's very restraint during the last series of wage negotiations was at the root of the trouble. An eighteen months' wages agreement had been negotiated at the time the steel industry was emerging from the mini-recession of 1966/67; no one then foresaw the unprecedented boom that was just around the corner or the pace at which the industry was about to go roaring ahead. The other union to be taken by surprise was the Mineworkers'. But if the two unions were caught off balance they regained command of the situation with exemplary expedition and found the alarmed employers' organisations more than willing to meet them halfway. Within a matter of days new wage agreements had been negotiated providing for increases in the most deserving cases of 11–14% and seldom averaging less than 7% to 8%. Industry very quickly returned to normal.

Both sides then set about ensuring that there would be no repetition. A clear warning had been given that was not to be ignored: the danger of perpetuating absurdly low wages during a period of boom could not have been more clearly demonstrated. The unwisdom of waiting for the expiry of wages agreements negotiated in wholly different circumstances twelve of fifteen months earlier was accepted by employers and unions alike. So, throughout the autumn, one union after another negotiated wage increases averaging around 10% and employers agreed readily enough, in the unusual circumstances, to waive their right to await the formal expiry dates of existing agreements.

During the few days in which the unions temporarily lost control it was noteworthy how ingrained habits of union discipline and custom persisted among the unofficial strikers; in some instances even the decision to return to work was taken by secret ballot. This stringent discipline was reminiscent of the strict naval discipline maintained among themselves by the Spithead mutineers in 1797! In such circumstances few opportunities were offered to left-wing extremists feverishly trying to add fuel to the flames. The young men who hurriedly motored from their universities to the scene of trouble were firmly told that they and their red flags and megaphones were not needed; the strikers preferred to make their own disciplined demonstration about the inadequacy of their wages without any supporting manifestation of student power. One interesting aspect of the whole affair was that the trouble occurred in those industries where the unions were already fully participating in management – and thus, as hostile critics did not hesitate to allege, had virtually lost their identity. *Paritätische Mitbestimmung* was evidently, they asserted, no panacea for industrial peace! Be that as it may, a few outspoken speakers, mainly Ministers and trade unionists (notably the Minister of Labour himself with a lifetime's experience of the Ruhr) were bold enough to draw attention to what was for West Germany almost a new phenomenon: it was the first time – outside the universities – that they had been confronted by the well-organised disruptive efforts of left-wing extremists (Maoists, Trotskyists, Anarchists, and other brands of Marxist), not officially affiliated to the Communist Party.

6

The Metal Workers' strike of 1971

In West Germany, as in other countries, it is most often the engineering industry – less often, the steel and coal industries – in which ripples of unrest tend most frequently to ruffle otherwise placid industrial waters. As mentioned in the previous chapter, the set-back of the 'wild week' of unofficial strikes in September 1969 was followed by a quick return to normal industrial relations, and wages settlements were reached in one industry after another with surprising ease. It was, oddly enough, the chemical industry in which difficulties next arose. A restrained kind of industrial action occurred in that industry in June 1971 and two or three very difficult weeks elapsed before a compromise settlement, involving a 7·8% increase, was reached.

The dispute had been followed with close attention by both sides of the metal industry (it had, indeed, features of unusual interest to which attention is drawn in the following chapter) and it was thought that it might well serve to induce the Metal Workers' Union (*IG Metall*) and the Engineering Employers' Association (*Gesamtmetall*) to set about drawing up a new agreement, on the expiry of their existing agreement in September, with a minimum of argument and vexatious discussion. Such hopes, however, were to be dashed.

The bargaining position

Although the union, particularly its top leadership, was anxious to avoid a clash, the same caution was not so evident on the part of the employers. They certainly adopted a decidedly uncompromising and inflexible attitude. Normally, negotiations get well under way before an agreement terminates but on this occasion the employers deferred serious discussions until well into October. The union, for bargaining purposes, had put forward a claim for a 10–11% increase. Some time elapsed before the employers made their counter offer and when it came it was as low as

4·5%. Having regard to other wages agreements negotiated during the year no one took this very seriously and it was generally assumed that the two sides would soon be settling for somewhere around 7%, i.e. a figure providing a small margin above current increases in the cost of living.

The union was in a difficult position. In West Germany, as elsewhere, left-wing activity on the shop-floor had recently been on the increase and the union was not unmindful of the way in which the little wave of unofficial strikes just two years earlier had revealed elements at work that it had not till then taken very seriously. It was only too well aware that if it accepted so poor an increase as 4·5% it would have to face great and quite understandable dissatisfaction on the part of many members who were already complaining about increases in the cost of living. Widespread dissatisfaction of this nature would provide trouble-makers with just the opportunity they had been looking for. The union's leader, Otto Brenner, a loyal member of the Social Democratic Party, had been trying ever since the formation of the Social Democrat/Free Democrat Coalition not to embarrass the Government either by making over-high wages demands or by getting involved in an industrial dispute.

The employers, for their part, without deliberately setting out to embarrass the Government, seem to have reached the conclusion that it was time to take a hard line without much regard to political repercussions; even a strike and lock-out might, they thought, be preferable to granting wages increases above the limit industry could in their opinion reasonably bear. They overlooked various public statements made by the union to the effect that the time for large wage increases had gone by. The issue between the two sides, each backed by a welter of economic data, resolved itself into this: what sort of increases were to be regarded as reasonable?

The motive behind the employers' tactics seems to have been the belief that, the longer they delayed a settlement, the more likely their appraisal of the economic situation would command general support. They had long been complaining, understandably enough, of the harmful effects of the international monetary uncertainties; the floating of the D-Mark at that time was, they alleged, seriously endangering industry's export competitiveness and the risk of an increasing rate of inflation was looming larger. Unfortunately, they over-exaggerated their case and – although this came at a later stage in the dispute – even went so far as to put a full-page advertisement in many newspapers painting an exaggeratedly gloomy picture of a country faced by imminent recession, with wage increases undermining its stability. It so happened that a report by the quasi-official Group of Economic Advisers (the *Sachverständigenrat*, usually known as the 'Five Wise Men'– who have already been referred to) had been saying much the same thing. The employers' statements nevertheless received a

derisive reception from the unions who had so often had to listen to the
sort of gloomy propaganda that:

> 'poured forth prophetic truths in awful strain,
> dark as the language of the Delphic fane'

They had come to regard such predictions as just part of the employers'
stock-in-trade at the bargaining table. When at long last the Jeremiads
began to acquire rather more significance they fell on deaf ears. Trade
unionists accepted the fact that the economy was cooling down but they
could see no evidence whatever that, as the employers alleged, a slump
was imminent. How could this be so, they argued, with 2·2 million foreign
workers at work and unemployment running at a mere 0·8%?

The breakdown of negotiations

In view of this difference of outlook it was not surprising that negotiations
began to break down in every 'Land' or region and recourse was soon
being made to the conciliation procedures that were part of the elaborate
cooling-off measures sensibly agreed on by the two sides following the
1963 strike. Unfortunately, the conciliation attempts on this most
important occasion failed conspicuously. Conciliators, like football
referees, are seldom to be envied, but their performances on this occasion
were lamentable. The Metal Workers' Union showed some disposition to
accept the solutions the conciliators put forward, however imperfect, but
the employers for their part turned down every proposal but one – that of
the Hamburg conciliator who suggested 6%. In the usual trouble spot,
North-Baden/North-Württemberg, everything was clearly going to turn on
shrewd and skilful conciliation. Here, however, as luck would have it, the
conciliator saw fit to couple his suggestion for an increase of 7·5% with a
maladroit proposal that the agreement should run for a mere seven
months. The union, with its eye on the 7·5% (and mindful that it is easier
to get a little more out of employers in the spring than in the autumn) was
prepared to accept. The employers, however, can hardly be blamed for
turning it down flat as it would have meant that they would have to go
through the long drawn-out agony of fresh wages negotiations all over
again the following spring.

It was ironic and singularly unfortunate that this, the most infelicitous
of the attempts at conciliation, should have related specifically to North-
Baden/North-Württemberg. This was a region still ruled over at that time
by the toughest of all the union's officials – a militant of the old school
who had never quite managed to rid himself of the conceptions of class
warfare he had assimilated in his earlier communist days. He happened to
be faced by an equally redoubtable opponent from Daimler-Benz, a man

moulded in the most rigid and inflexible tradition of Germany's 'manager' class and often referred to as 'IG Metall's bogey man'. It was said of them both that they took pride in their reputation of being 'as hard as the metal they work on'. They had fought each other for years and had acquired remarkable dexterity in brinkmanship. This time, however, they went too near the edge and precipitated the first dispute of any consequence to take place in Germany since the 1963 strike (which also, it is unnecessary to recall, took place in Baden-Württemberg).

The regional union official referred to was due to retire within a few months at the age of 65. He had recently been making little attempt to control his temperamental outbursts, particularly as these increased his popularity among the more militant elements in Stuttgart. It seems almost as if he had made up his mind to celebrate the end of his trade union career by smiting the bosses hip and thigh. After the breakdown of conciliation, the dispute started in much the same way as in 1963. First of all the workers were called out in Mannheim, Stuttgart and Neckarsulm, a move promptly countered by the employers with a lock-out that immediately put 360,000 men out of work. Although a lock-out is a legitimate weapon it is generally held to be brutal; there were those within the employers' ranks who were uneasy about the cost and destructive power of such an 'atomic' weapon. Employers were soon losing DM70 millions per working day; their Federation, *Gesamtmetall*, was in addition paying out some DM16 millions to its member firms involved in the lock-out. The union, for its part, instead of paying strike monies to a strictly limited number of its members at selected firms, found itself having to make payment to all its locked-out members throughout North-Baden/North-Württemberg. The average union member was at that time entitled to receive at least DM40 (say about £5) a day; this involved union funds in a loss of DM10 millions every day the strike lasted.

The State's strict neutrality in refraining from financing strikers and leaving it entirely to a union to support its militant members has the advantage of ensuring that disputes of this nature, even when restricted in scope, are never taken lightly. It is in everybody's interest not to let the dispute go on a day longer than necessary. The expense, alongside such other good reasons as the vociferous public disapprobation, drove Brenner and his opposite number, van Hüllen, to try and make a top level attempt to find a solution. They met at Wiesbaden on 26th November and quickly agreed on another conciliation attempt, this time under the chairmanship of the conciliator who had helped to settle the recent chemical dispute. Everyone was at pains meanwhile to try and make sure that industrial action did not start in any of the other Länder, although nothing could be done about the factories that were already being affected by the non-delivery of components from Stuttgart and Mannheim. The negotiators elsewhere in Germany quietly watched the progress of the dispute in North-Baden/North-Württemburg. Its outcome was obviously going to serve as the basis for settlements in all the other 'Länder'. Neither the employers' confederation nor the union wished to perpetrate the folly of letting the dispute spread.

The conciliation attempts

The new conciliation attempt started off in an atmosphere of restrained optimism. After five days of fruitless discussion, however, it became evident that the conciliator had not only failed to persuade either side to budge an inch but had, it would seem, even driven them farther apart. At this worst of all possible moments the Federal Chancellor intervened. He invited the conciliator to fly to Bonn together with the two negotiating teams. The atmosphere by now prevailing was such that the two sides chose not to travel together but flew from Stuttgart in separate planes, the employers in one and the trade unionists in the other. The futility of their final session in the Chancellor's office was farcical and the flight to Bonn had merely queered the pitch for any further political intervention.

A most interesting situation had been reached. Just as in 1963 (despite brave words about 'Tarif-Autonomie' and 'the only useful form of Government intervention is non-intervention') the weary antagonists would by now have been thankful for the appearance of a *deus ex machina*, even in the form of the Economics Minister. Had the invitation to come to Bonn been made two days later it might conceivably have served a useful purpose – although it would still have been felt to be an odd proceeding on the part of the Federal Government to approach regional negotiators over the heads of national negotiators. At this awkward moment the conciliator unfortunately let it become known that he had recommended a wages increase of 7·5% coupled with a 40% improvement in respect of the 'thirteenth month', i.e., the Christmas bonus; for full measure he had suggested lump sum payments for the last three months of 1971 as yet another sop to the union. This seemed to employers an odd sort of conciliation when the conciliator suddenly came down wholly on the side of one of the contending parties! Their initial angry bewilderment was succeeded by cynical gloom. They were heard applying to conciliators the hard old saying about doctors: 'The best is the one you run for and cannot find' and let it be known that they had come to regard a conciliator as a 'middleman who bamboozles one party and plunders the other'.

The dispute had by now developed in such a way that the employers, at least, had come to assume that anything that could go wrong would go wrong. It hardly helped them to reflect that they had in large part brought their difficulties on themselves. They had begun by having the better cards and had played them ruthlessly without heed to the union's predicament. They had ignored Otto Brenner's tentative advances and done little to prevent the dispute, confident that this time they would 'teach the union a lesson'. Another mischance was that, in the middle of the dispute, Parliament decided, contrary to all expectation, to delay the passing of the new Works Constitution Law – a step which the unions at once interpreted as due to evil machinations on the part of the employers; the marked deterioration in the relations between the DGB and the Employers National Confederation (BDA) that followed had, of course, its side effects on the Engineering Employers' Association (*Gesamtmetall*) and further aggravated the situation.

A fresh disaster then overtook the employers from a wholly unexpected quarter – from the Federal Institute of Labour in Nürnberg (the *Bundesanstalt für Arbeit*, the quasi-governmental organisation responsible for the national employment exchange service). What follows appears to be worth narrating because of the light it throws on the financial aspects of a strike in West Germany. In 1969 some subtle changes had been made in basic legislation concerning the non-payment of unemployment money to strikers; in the absence of a strike there had never till now been a chance to test out the effect of these changes. The engineering dispute at last provided the occasion. The President of the Federal Institute of Labour (vulnerable to criticism in socialist trade union circles because of his membership of the Conservative opposition party (the CDU)) took a step which was to prove unfortunate. In the urgency of the moment he issued an instruction to employment exchanges – without first consulting the tripartite governing body (*Vorstand*) as it was alleged he ought to have done – to make no payments to those 'indirectly' concerned with the strike. This was the signal for a first-class row. The strike and lock-out in North-Baden/North-Württemberg had been causing people in other parts of Germany to lose their jobs, at least for the time being. No one for a moment disputed that men and women employed in another industry, e.g., in a tyre factory, were entitled to receive unemployment money but the President's instruction apparently precluded payment of unemployment money to anyone who was laid-off anywhere in the engineering industry owing to lack of essential components. Within a few days of the instruction being promulgated the issue was hurriedly brought before the Federal Institute's tripartite Governing Body and revoked; following angry discussion, the governmental representatives voted alongside the workers' representatives, thus forming a majority in opposition to the employers' representatives. The revoking of the instruction meant that those indirectly affected by the strike in the metal industry in all parts of Germany, apart from the North-Baden/North-Württemberg area, were able after all to make a claim to unemployment money.

That the receipt of contradictory instructions within a few days caused enormous difficulties to employment exchanges is neither here nor there. In itself the revised instruction could hardly be challenged as it was clearly aimed at helping only those who were taking no part whatsoever in the dispute and could well be regarded as its innocent victims. But what really mattered was that, at a time when passions were running high, yet another bone of contention had been tossed between employers and union. The employers could only see the matter from their point of view and unwisely announced that they would leave no stone unturned in getting the President's original ruling reinstated. Leaving aside the legal and constitutional complexities involved, the reason why the employers were so upset by the revised instruction was because it suddenly eased union funds at the moment when the dispute was reaching its climax. Overnight the union was set free of an obligation to support its members all over the country who had lost their employment as an indirect consequence of the dispute; it had now only to concern itself with paying its membership in North-Baden/North-Württemberg and was thus in a much better position financially for prolonging the struggle.

The situation now reached in West Germany's industrial relations was the gravest at any time since the War. Although the Schleswig-Holstein strike of 1957 had lasted for the exceptional length of four months it had affected but a few firms and had been very strictly localised; it had given rise to nothing like the concern the present dispute was causing. It had at last become clear to the protagonists themselves that the only hope of ending the dispute would be to return to the conference table. Their professional pride – particularly that of those in the head offices – had been wounded by finding themselves stigmatised on all hands as incompetent bunglers. The negotiators in Baden-Württemberg were now very firmly prodded by their head offices to make a final attempt to sort out the mess into which excessive obstinacy, negotiating inflexibility, maladroit intervention – and, it must be added, a quite exceptional amount of bad luck – had got them into.

Optimism – and concessions

There was at once a new note of optimism. This time it was justified: both sides were at last equally intent on getting the miserable affair over and done with. The hard-pressed employers had now been brought to the point of making concessions they would not have entertained a week earlier. Fourteen hours' intensive discussion resulted in agreement on the following terms:

7·5% increase from 1st January 1972. Payment before Christmas of a lump sum of DM 180 to all employees (DM 60 for each of the three months following expiry of the previous agreement in September). A gradual stepping up of the '13 month' payment so as to reach 40% by 1st January 1974.

With its customary good sense the German newspaper press, irrespective of Party sympathies, took the line that there had been neither victors nor vanquished. The employers, however, as they bound up their wounds, must have been ruefully conscious that the 'victory' which a few of them claimed was of the sort associated with the Western Front during the 1914–18 war – enormous losses had been incurred merely to regain ground held a few weeks earlier. How much better it would have been to take the 7·3% settlement the union had been willing to accept a few weeks back! Fortunately, no responsible union officials outside Baden-Württemberg saw fit to crow over what was for them the surprisingly successful outcome of a decidedly distasteful and rather silly business. The discomfiture of *Gesamtmetall* was all very well but wise trade unionists, like many an employer, had been aghast at the prospect of the dispute spreading to the whole engineering industry. It might well have left a legacy of bitterness that would have taken years to overcome.

Lessons of the strike

The history of this, West Germany's most serious dispute, has been set out at this length on account of the light it throws on important aspects of the country's industrial relations. It is when things go thoroughly wrong, as they did on this occasion, that the strength and weaknesses of a good system of industrial relations can best be studied. One significant outcome was that it brought home to employers and unions alike the impossibility these days of waging industrial warfare in the automobile industry on a purely localised front. In the 1963 dispute the effects had been strictly limited to Baden-Württemberg; this time the whole German motor-car industry was affected. The 1971 affair revealed the enormous strides in rationalisation and specialisation that had been made since 1963; the production processes of one firm had become inextricably interlocked with those of another. In 1963 the Daimler-Benz plant at Mannheim was virtually self-sufficient; it had now become largely an assembly works for parts manufactured elsewhere. A working agreement between MAN and Daimler-Benz meant that difficulties at one firm would in future immediately affect the other. Two days after the dispute brought the Stuttgart radiator specialists Behr to a halt, shortages of radiators began affecting firms hundreds of kilometres away. All this sort of thing had long been familiar enough to strike-ridden Britain but it came as a sudden shock to West Germany. Rightly or wrongly, the Germans had been increasingly attributing Britain's unemployment and increasing economic and financial difficulties to its apparently incessant strikes; it was a major topic of newspaper articles. Uneasy voices began to ask: 'Can it be that we in Germany are about to go the same way?'

Much uneasiness was also felt about the possibility that the dispute – particularly the bitterness to which the lock-out had given rise – might impair the excellent atmosphere prevailing between management and labour in so many German undertakings. On the other hand, there was much quiet satisfaction about the truly exemplary way in which picketing had been carried out; discipline and good humour had prevailed and there had been a remarkable absence of unpleasant incident. This could be ascribed to the excellence of the union's organisation and to the relative ineffectiveness of Communists and left-wing extremists in Baden-Württemberg – an area traditionally somewhat militant but, unlike the Ruhr, never much inclined to Communism. A great deal of mischief-making had, as the union well knew, been going on in Land Nordrhein/Westfalen and above all in the Ruhr where the printing presses of the various Marxist organisations had been working night and day turning out floods of inflammatory pamphlets urging the workers to smash the capitalist bosses. The language used in these pamphlets echoed, with hardly a change of syllable, the uncompromising doctrines of Marx, Engels, Liebknecht, Bebel and Kautsky. Their exhortations fell for the most part on deaf ears as German trade unionism has remained faithful to the policy enunciated by Eduard Bernstein after his retreat from Marxist extremism, i.e. that of not seeking to bring about the collapse of the existing order through revolution but rather to achieve socialism by slow, constructive evolution. Although the Marxist campaign had achieved little success the employers – who must have known that something of this kind might happen in what used to be a pre-war trouble centre – seem to have been decidedly unwise in driving the union into a militancy which, with local exceptions, was none of its choice.

The dispute, though localised in one region and one industry, left everyone concerned in a decidedly chastened mood. Both sides had been widely, unsparingly and, on the whole, justifiably criticised. For too many years they had been acquiring the habit of indulging in a sort of ritual war dance in respect of their annual wage negotiations. Admittedly, they had nearly always reached a sensible enough settlement in the end, but was it really necessary, as one newspaper put it, to keep on imitating in the 1970s the haggling processes of an oriental bazaar? Some likened the annual encounters between IG Metall and *Gesamtmetall* to a stylised nineteenth-century duel. First the challenge, followed by the proffering of a face-saving formula, its rejection and formal acceptance of the challenge; next, the loading of the pistols, the pacing-out of the duelling ground, the taking-up of positions and finally, just as the word to fire is about to be given, the precipitate intervention of outsiders – often in the shape of high authority – rushing up to call the whole thing off. Something rather like this had been going on for too many years in the engineering industry and the question being asked everywhere was whether it was still necessary to adopt such elaborate and time-wasting processes of negotiation; why follow the techniques of attrition, challenge and counter-challenge, when a settlement has got to be reached in the long run by negotiation anyway? (A truth, it might be added, that had long been recognised and put into effective practice throughout Austria and in most other industries in West Germany.)

There was no longer any need for the two sides in the engineering industry to demonstrate, by periodic displays of strength and martial valour, how well organised and powerful they were: everybody knew that already. It was made clear to the self-styled 'pace-makers in wage negotiations' that the country expected them to do a great deal better on the next occasion. Put bluntly, most Germans had come to assume that their industrialists and trade unionists had grown out of this old-fashioned type of industrial dispute; it came as a shock and surprise to find that they had not. 'A hark-back to Grandpa's style of wage negotiation' was a typical comment on the strike.

But for one thing at least the two sides were clearly not to blame: the extraordinary failure of the elaborate conciliation procedures they had spent so much time and effort in developing. One lesson to be derived from this was that no amount of legal acumen will ever take the place of sound human understanding and the 'horse sense' without which a conciliator cannot effectively conciliate. It is only fair to point out that this was one of the very rare occasions when the conciliation methods practised in Germany have come to grief.

Such, briefly, were the German reactions to an unhappy affair which left those concerned somewhat shamefaced. To put the matter in perspective, it must be remembered that this was only the second dispute of any gravity to occur in the West German engineering industry since the war and that each had been confined to a localised front. In general, despite occasional stresses and strains and some warlike noises, the industry's record had been one of uninterrupted industrial peace, with production mounting from month to month and year to year. However tedious the long drawn-out annual wage negotiations had often appeared to onlookers, the two sides had almost invariably contrived to reach reasonable enough settlements in the end.

A few further comments seem called for. The unusual bitterness of this particular struggle was undoubtedly due to the importance attached to the issues at stake. The engineering employers had attempted to make a stand, not only on behalf of their own industry but of industry as a whole, against wage demands of more than 6% – demands which, they seem to have been convinced, could no longer be met even in so flourishing an economy as that of the Federal Republic without courting the risk of losing export markets and, still more serious, giving a further fillip to a marked inflationary trend. That in the end they conceded as much as 7·5% was undoubtedly a withdrawal from their position and they were obliged to make a concession to the union on another point of principle, namely, that wage increases should, in times of exceptional prosperity, do something more than just keep pace with increases in the cost of living.

The dispute also serves to draw attention to another merit of the German system of negotiation. It firmly guarantees industrial peace for periods of twelve months at a time. Following the termination of the dispute, employers could confidently go ahead with their export programmes in the certain knowledge of being able to meet every delivery date. Neither side has ever broken an agreement – not at least since the quite exceptional and very controversial instance back in 1957 when the exemplary damages awarded against the Metal Workers' Union by the Federal Labour Court emphasised once and for all that contractual obligations are binding on unions just as much as on employers.

Perhaps the most significant outcome of the affair, however, was the way in which it strengthened belief in what is held in the Federal Republic to be one of the fundamental economic facts of life – that it is the uninterrupted productivity of firms and workers that has made West Germany more successful than any other major western European country in the fight against inflation and in keeping its currency stable. No industrial disputes worthy of the name have since taken place apart from a series of troublesome 'warning strikes' organised by the Union of Workers in Public Services, Transport and Communications early in 1974 and a strike and lock-out of printing workers in May 1976 that prevented most German newspapers from appearing and gave rise to much hostile public comment. Short and sharp 'warning strikes', attributable mainly to the difficulties that arise during a period of economic recession, have occasioned most of the ripples on the generally placid industrial waters during these last two years. Such strikes seldom lasted more than fifteen minutes or half-an-hour, although one went on for as long as four days. There is, of course, always an exception to prove the rule and the exception came from an apparently never-ending dispute over redundancies at a Westfalen cement factory between an obstinate employer and his equally obstinate employees (150 of them) – watched from all over Germany for over twelve months with not a little consternation. But in general there were fewer stoppages of work in 1975 than in 1974 — indeed, the total number of working days lost throughout the year amounted to only 68,700.

7

The dispute in the Chemical Industry
in 1971

The preceding chapter went into considerable detail in analysing the gravest and most unhappy dispute in the history of post-war German industrial relations. This was on account of the light it throws on the operation of trade unionism in adverse circumstances. The dispute followed close on the heels of another dispute – that in the chemical industry – which is also worth following because it emphasises some other aspects of post-war German trade unionism.

It has already been mentioned that when the Chemical Workers' Union put forward its claim, this followed a whole series of wage claims negotiated during the preceding months with very little friction (apart from quite minor local difficulties in the textile and clothing industries). The unions, despite their unwillingness formally to accept the Economic and Finance Minister's wage guidelines in which he advocated the limitation of wages increases to not more than 7–8%, had been consistently negotiating settlements in remarkably close accord with the Government's wishes. These settlements were briefly as follows: As from 1st January 1971 an increase of 8% had come into force for the railwaymen, followed by 7% for the postal workers. The Printers' Union then negotiated a settlement of 9% as from 1st February and shortly afterwards the construction workers accepted an increase of 7·9% to take effect from 1st May. In April the coalmining industry had settled for 7·3%, the banking industry for 7·9%, and the insurance industry, early in May, for 7·7%. The picture thus presented was that of a trade union movement showing remarkable restraint during a period of quite exceptional economic prosperity, hardly rivalled by any other country before or since.

Financial difficulties in the chemical industry
It had, however, become obvious that a settlement in the chemical

industry might be unusually difficult to reach. This industry, unlike any other major West German industry, was after a period of ten years' continuous expansion, now facing genuine financial difficulties and experiencing an appreciable, even if temporary, slowing down of growth. Profits had begun to drop sharply as the industry, so largely dependent on exports, began to feel the effects of the revaluation of the Deutsche Mark. The situation took a sudden turn for the worse when the Mark was floated on 10th May 1971.

The Chemical Workers' Union was not unaware of the financial difficulties facing the industry. It blamed the employers, however, for bringing about a situation that, in its opinion, need never have arisen. It held that the industry had not only been ill-advised in its investment policy but had been misguided in seeking to build up its productive capacity of man-made fibres at a time when patent rights were about to expire. Moreover, despite the financial losses to which these mistakes had given rise, excellent dividends were still being paid by the major concerns, i.e. Bayer 16%, Hoechst 20%, and BASF (*Badische Anilin und Soda Fabrik*) 22%. The union was therefore disinclined to take the statement of the Managing Director of one of the largest chemical undertakings very seriously when he announced to shareholders that the profit situation had become so grave that chemical companies were really hardly in a position to make any wage increases at all. When he added that 20% dividends would go on being paid it was not surprising that the union reacted angrily. If the industry could continue, while in financial doldrums, to go on making dividend payments of this nature, this afforded clear proof, it argued, that there was adequate money in the kitty to permit wages to be raised. This brought a new factor into the familiar wages round. Up till now wage claims, in so far as they had not been fully covered by productivity increases, had been met by automatically passing on the increased costs to the consumer. The union knew that this easy solution was no longer within the industry's grasp but argued that the time had come, instead, for the very generous dividends to be cut back a little to permit the labour force to be rewarded more adequately.

The steps towards strike action

The Chemical Workers' Union had for long had the reputation of sharing with the Printers' Union a position on the far left-wing of the sixteen Unions affiliated to the DGB. The Metal Workers' Union had, it was true, some militant branches but, in general, it had come to be regarded as a little to the right of the Chemical Workers'. Despite some decidedly radical elements within its ranks, however, the Chemical Workers' Union had shown no more tendency to act irresponsibly than any other German trade union. The dispute that was developing was, in fact, spoken of as the first strike the industry had had for fifty years. Although that is not quite correct, its record had certainly been a remarkably good one and even the quite insignificant strikes that had occasionally occurred had been associated not with pay demands but with legitimate questions of principle. The union's reputation for left-wing radicalism was derived, in part at least, from the rough-hewn personality of the man who had led it from the time of its re-founding after the War until his retirement at the union's 1969 Congress when he was succeeded by a man of very different stamp, Karl Hauenschild. Hauenschild is of the modern manager type beginning to characterise German trade unionism. He possesses, in common with some of the other leaders of German trade unions (like Loderer, for example, successor to Otto Brenner as head of I. G. Metall) qualities so outstanding that he could be entrusted with the running of almost any of Germany's large industrial concerns. His attitude in respect of his own industry had been expressed time and again in one of his favourite phrases: 'We have no intention of slaughtering the cow that gives us its milk.' He has stated his general outlook in the following words: 'Trade union policy is the art of the possible. It can exert an influence on a Government's policy but must subordinate itself to the majority situation and party relationships as they exist in Parliament and Government.'

A new undercurrent of unrest was already in 1969 becoming detectable among German workers, following its marked manifestations in Italy, France and Britain. Activists were evidently attempting to use trade unionism not merely as a means of discomfiting managements but of hastening the end of the capitalist system. The new trend, though a good deal less significant in West Germany than elsewhere, had in the opinion of many prominent personalities competent to judge been revealed by the little outbreak of 'September strikes' that took place that year. That the Communist Party was increasing its activities was being loudly affirmed by many prominent Social Democrats. Most German trade union leaders, however, were less concerned by open Communist activity than by the subtle influence of 'ex-Communists' and a heterogeneous collection of various types of Marxist who, although small in numbers, were displaying great skill in their use of insidious methods; a phenomenon new to post-war Germany, but one that brought back some unhappy memories, was the way they did not shrink from using violence on occasion. Groups of this kind can cause a good deal more trouble than their insignificant numbers would seem to warrant. Hauenschild found himself in much the same situation as had confronted his colleague Otto Brenner of the Metal Workers' Union: if he failed to assert himself adequately and gave any appearance of yielding to the employers his leadership would unquestionably be challenged by the more militant elements within his union. It was unfortunate that the obduracy of the employers gave him little choice but to adopt a militant attitude.

British employers and employers' confederations have sometimes been criticised in Germany for their weakness, if not pusillanimity, in yielding too readily to exorbitant wage demands. Clearly there are occasions when an employers' confederation has no option but to close its ranks and stand firm in the face of such demands. But that an unduly unyielding attitude also has its dangers was exemplified by the tactics adopted on this occasion by the German employers' confederation – the *Arbeitsring der Arbeitgeberverbände der Deutschen Chemischen Industrie e.V.* and its sister organisation, the *Verband der Chemischen Industrie e.V.* Both had for many months been known to be preparing for a show-down if necessary. The union, thus forewarned, had set about perfecting its own mobilisation arrangements and working out new tactical methods in the event of negotiations breaking down. For this purpose the union had an advantage not possessed by any of the other fifteen affiliated DGB unions. Owing to an amendment made to its constitution at Wiesbaden in 1963 (the celebrated 'Section 16' – the subject of intense and continuing controversy), its leadership was able – unlike any of the other affiliated DGB unions – to call for strike action without first holding a secret ballot. This union is thus the one exception to the procedure outlined in Chapter 4, being in a position to carry out sudden selected strikes whenever it chooses. Such strikes are regarded by employers in the Federal Republic, unaccustomed to this sort of thing, as an unscrupulous type of guerrilla warfare and the *Arbeitsring* was prompt to challenge its operation in the Land where its legality seemed most open to question, i.e. Nordrhein Westfalen – only to have its case adjourned to the end of July and thus postponed until the present fray would be over.

At the early stages of the negotiations, when argument was still rational and more or less objective, the employers seemed unwilling to budge beyond 5·5% as a maximum. It was not long, however, before the arguments got more and more heated until, at least at the regional level, the not altogether unfamiliar situation was being reached that the antagonists 'having made up their minds were prepared no longer to be confused by facts'. The union's attitude had at least the merit of a certain disarming simplicity: 'make us an offer at the level of the Government's wage guidelines and we will be happy to resume negotiations'. Belatedly the employers put up their offer but still only to a maximum of 6·5% – a figure well below the level of the guidelines.

Towards the end of May the dispute grew more serious and one attempt at conciliation after another was tried and failed. Things then seemed to take a turn for the better. The two sides in the District (*Bezirk*) of Rheinland-Pfalz-Saar agreed on 24th May to a wages increase which, related to a ten months' period of validity, worked out at 7·8%. As this Bezirk contained Germany's second largest chemical undertaking, BASF, there seemed reason to hope that such an example of sweet reason would find its emulators. On the contrary, as bad luck would have it, on the same day as the Rheinland-Pfalz-Saar agreement was reached a further attempt at conciliation in Hessen broke down. This seems to have induced employers in Nordrhein-Westfalen to make no improvement on their own offer which was also well below the level of the wage guidelines. Hauenschild now went on record as saying that the chemical workers had a right to receive at least the same increases as had recently been negotiated in the mining, clothing, and banking industries. At the same time the union made the gesture of reducing its pay claim to 9% from an original apparently excessive demand (put forward, however, purely for bargaining purposes) of 13%, thus making it easier for the employers to move away from their own rigid bargaining position.

The employers decided to stand firm, however, and so, by the end of the first week in June, the union began to organise protests which it followed up with selective strikes. At the outset, the protests took the form of orderly rallies and demonstrations and short stoppages of work lasting only an hour or so. The hope was that these protests would alarm employers and induce them to improve their offer. Production was not affected at this stage but when the employers still made no concessions and final deadlock was reached in yet another *Bezirk* (Hamburg) the union decided to intensify its campaign. The new phase was to be one of lightning stoppages which might last a day or even longer. These stoppages occurred for the most part at small concerns and many of them involved, in practice, hours rather than days, a typical technique being to extend the morning breakfast-break by up to two hours. The aim was to put a maximum of nerve strain on employers while still avoiding serious disruptions of production. This type of warning strike was not always effective, as old habits of friendly co-operation between management and men sometimes die hard. At least one union representative is known to have advised his firm of the time and duration of a 'surprise impromptu demonstration stoppage' arranged to take place the next day.

The start of militant action

Once militant action starts, it is only natural for radical extremists (the *Radikalinskis*) to try and make a difficult situation worse. It was not long before responsible officials of the union began to find themselves in rather a fix. On the one hand, appreciable numbers of the membership were showing little enthusiasm for the dispute while, on the other, extreme left-wing elements were endeavouring to incite much more drastic action in support of demands considerably in excess of those countenanced by the union. Ugly incidents began to arise where workers were prevented from going to work by over-zealous pickets. Some observers who had been studying recent strikes in Britain pointed out that these encounters were on a pattern that had been tried out not long before at Halewood, while other incidents bore a marked resemblance to the types of violence associated with the Pilkington strike the previous year. Just as at St. Helen's, some of the pickets using physical force against 'strike-breakers' were not employees of the firm at all but men infiltrated from other localities for the express purpose of stirring up trouble. Members of the Communist Party were, as usual, on these occasions busy handing out their provocative leaflets but the extent of direct Communist influence seems to have been exaggerated by employers; the most direct intimidation was found by the union to come not from the openly declared Communists but from other types of Marxist not formal members of the German Communist Party (the DKP).

Against a background of demonstrations and short lightning strikes throughout June, discussions between the two sides were kept going but came to nothing. Production was still hardly being affected. Small firms (where, oddly enough, quite contrary to normal experience, the *Radikalinskis* were causing more trouble than in the big undertakings) were the main victims, but even their losses were for the most part not so great that they could not quickly be made good by subsequent overtime. By the end of the month, out of a total of at least a thousand undertakings only fifty had been affected by strike action and only 30,000 workers out of a possible 400,000 had been involved. But any further escalation would start having serious effects on production. This consideration seems to have been much in the mind of Hauenschild who, like other German trade union leaders, had often made it clear that he was as fully aware as the employers of the effect disputes may have on export competitiveness, to say nothing of devitalising the economy. Locked in a very painful clinch, the adversaries were embarrassed by cries of (so to speak) 'hit him harder' from ringside spectators. The Engineering Employers' Confederation (*Gesamtmetall*), in particular, watched their colleagues in the chemical industry bearing the brunt of a battle which, if successfully fought, would, they hoped, make it easier for them to resist the wages demands they were shortly expecting to be lodged by the Metal Workers' Union.

By the end of June, however, both the *Arbeitsring* and the Union were aware that morale was weakening. Individual undertakings were showing a marked tendency to reach 9% settlements with local union officials; prompt application of the penalty of immediate expulsion of the undertakings concerned from the *Arbeitsring* afforded no guarantee that other firms might not follow suit. A growing lack of enthusiasm was being displayed, too, by many workers as the dispute dragged on, particularly by those in the larger firms. Reluctant strikers were asking why the secret ballot procedure had not been put into operation and there was some reason to suspect that, had a ballot been held, the necessary 75% majority for strike action might not have been forthcoming.

Hopes, therefore, ran high when on 30th June the Social Democrat Minister of Labour in Land Nordrhein-Westfalen made what seemed a well-timed further attempt at conciliation. Things did not go at all well, however. The weary protagonists had already spent the best part of seventeen hours 'baling out water with sieves' when, at the very last moment, the employers pushed up their offer from 6·5% and offered two alternatives: either 7·5% as a lump sum payment to cover the two months' gap between the last and the new agreement or, alternatively, a straightforward increase of 7·8%. Had the offer been made a fortnight – or even a few hours - earlier, it might well have been accepted on the spot. By this time, however, the union representatives were hardly in a frame of mind to agree to anything and at 5 a.m. on 1st July the perplexed and angry negotiators left the offices of the Ministry without having achieved anything. Angry recriminations followed, more particularly between the *Arbeitsring* and the Minister, in the course of which the latter implied that the employers were politically motivated in declining to offer 8% as he had told them to do – thus effectively ruling himself out of playing any further conciliatory role.

Government intervention

But the absurdity of continuing a dispute when the disputants were now separated by a difference of a mere ·08% had become apparent to all, apart from the usual hard core of shopfloor militants and a few obdurate employers. The Federal Government rightly judged the time ripe for intervention – the more so as it had reason to fear that the next stage would be an escalation affecting quite a number of chemical works within a specific region or even the temporary closure of some large undertaking. The two sides, jealous of their *Tarif-Autonomie* are normally hostile to Government intervention; the unions have always made it clear that they resent this just as much if it comes from a Social Democratic Government as from a Conservative Government. But commonsense could not but suggest to them that, on this occasion, the Government's good offices afforded the best prospect of finding a face-saving solution. When, therefore, a proposal was made by the Federal Chancellor's office that the President of the Federal Social Court should mediate, the offer was taken up with alacrity.

The new mediation attempt got off to a good start in a much better atmosphere. The principals – Hauenschild and the head of the *Arbeitsring* – had at last been drawn in and had clearly made up their mind to find a solution where their subordinates had failed. The outcome of the 21 hours' tough and intensive negotiations that ensued was a thoroughly sensible compromise. Neither side could be said to have won – each had to make concessions. A 7·8% wage increase was agreed with provision for the payment of a lump sum of DM60 to bridge the gap between the old and the new agreement. The pill was sweetened a little for the union by a provision that the 'Christmas gratification' would be improved step by step to bring a 'thirteen months' annual salary into operation by the end of 1974. The employers agreed to discontinue any further legal action against the union, apart from testing out the important point of principle that emerged from the strike: can a strike be regarded as legal if it is called without first taking a secret ballot?

In many countries the dispute would have been regarded as very small beer. The possibility of fairly wide strike action had, however, been sufficiently imminent to alarm public opinion: press, radio and television dealt at length, day after day, with the familiar topic of whether the Federal Republic was going to go the way of other strike-prone countries. The Metal Workers' dispute later in the year was to redouble these anxieties.

1971 thus afforded the unusual spectacle of two disputes in a country grown accustomed to an industrial peace comparable to that prevailing in Austria or Switzerland. One important lesson, however, could be drawn from what had just happened in the chemical industry. It demonstrated the way in which a gifted, highly responsible trade union leader, free of ideological predilections, can use the advantages which his position gives him to gain better wages and conditions for his members without injuring the industry from which they derive their livelihood. Hauenschild had contended with inflexible opposition on the part of the employers while simultaneously exposed to a harassing fire from a radical and, in some instances, politically-motivated element on the shop floor, intent only on short-term gains. The dispute ended in such a way as to constitute a triumph for the union's top leadership and furnished yet another proof of how fortunate West Germany has been in the way its unions are led. Many opportunities had presented themselves to mischief makers but, apart from the few nasty incidents created by the pickets, they had achieved nothing. But if the union's top leadership had not handled the situation time and again in such a way as to prevent it getting out of hand, the tail might have wagged the dog and West Germany's chemical industry, at a time of competitive weakness, could have been dealt a very hard knock. The whole affair could be regarded as justifying the view of those who acclaim the wisdom of German trade union leadership in resolutely refusing to allow too much power to be delegated to the shop floor. As it was, there was more than an occasional hint of what can happen – in a union not quite so well organised as the Metal Workers'– if the authority of local officials is insufficient to enable them to exercise a restraining influence over shop-floor militants.

Strike money entitlement

As it throws some light on the finances of a medium-sized German trade union the following table has been prepared setting out the strike monies to which members of the Chemical Workers' Union were entitled, in relation to their membership dues.

Contribution Class	Monthly Contribution	Strike monies payable weekly after a Membership of			
		3 months	1 year	3 years	
1	3.50	27.00	33.00	36.00	DM
2	4.00	33.00	36.00	42.00	DM
3	4.50	36.00	42.00	48.00	DM
4	5.00	42.00	48.00	54.00	DM
5	5.50	45.00	51.00	57.00	DM
6	6.00	48.00	57.00	63.00	DM
7	6.50	54.00	60.00	69.00	DM
8	7.00	57.00	66.00	75.00	DM
9	7.50	60.00	69.00	78.00	DM
10	8.00	66.00	75.00	84.00	DM
11	8.50	69.00	81.00	90.00	DM
12	9.00	75.00	84.00	96.00	DM
13	10.00	81.00	93.00	105.00	DM
14	11.00	90.00	102.00	117.00	DM
15	12.00	99.00	111.00	126.00	DM
16	13.00	105.00	120.00	138.00	DM
17	15.00	123.00	141.00	159.00	DM

The last three columns relate to weekly payments.
Alongside the strike payments specified above, extra family allowances were paid by the Union as follows: Wife – DM10 a week. Children (not gainfully occupied) – DM5 a week.

In view of the picketing incidents alluded to during the dispute, it may be found helpful to refer to *Appendix II* (on Strike Law in the Federal Republic) which contains a short summary of the law in regard to picketing.

8

The Construction Workers' Union

German trade unionists have frequently expressed their surprise at the attitude of their British colleagues to industrial strife. It is naturally taken for granted that industrial dissension is at times inevitable (witness the disputes dealt with in the two preceding chapters) and a strong trade union movement must unquestionably be ready to grasp the strike weapon when occasion demands. But German observers often remark that Britain seems to have acquired the habit of striking first and discussing afterwards. The German view is that the strength and unity of a trade union movement is best displayed by the infrequency with which industrial disputes arise — and they point to countries such as Switzerland, Austria and Sweden in support of this contention.

The avoidance of industrial disputes

A good example of how this view can be put into practice is to be found in the recent history of the Construction Workers' Union (*Industriegewerkschaft Bau, Steine, Erden*) although the Textile Workers' Union (*Gewerkschaft Textil-Bekleidung*) might almost equally well be taken. The Construction Workers' Union embarked on its new course when Herr Georg Leber (later to hold ministerial office) took over the leadership of the union in 1957. Leber may have run his union, as is sometimes alleged, in the manner of a benevolent despot but the course he set for it has been one of uninterrupted success and of enormous benefit to the workers in the construction industry. Real wages went up by more than two-and-a-half times in twenty years, the working week was reduced from 48 hours to 40 hours, and working conditions were improved out of all knowledge.

At the time Herr Leber took over the leadership of his union, it was already becoming clear that the balance of power in industrial conflict in most western European countries was swinging from capital to labour.

Leber made up his mind to see what could be achieved by co-operation rather than confrontation. He saw no reason why, to use current jargon, the two sides should live in a state of hostile symbiosis and considered the time had come when

> 'all things invite
> to peaceful counsels, and the settled state
> of order'.

The change in union attitude very quickly brought about a corresponding change in management attitudes and, as the atmosphere improved, the two sides began to work increasingly closely together to try to remove, or at least to improve, the unpleasant and uncongenial conditions long accepted as unavoidable in the construction industries. Leber launched a campaign to show that frost and snow were giving rise to ten weeks' compulsory unemployment every year and set about, in close co-operation with the other side, to devise ways and means of keeping employment going even throughout the conditions of a German winter. The result is that building work now continues during January and February under weather conditions – far worse than anything ever experienced in the southern part of Britain – that would formerly have been held to make work impossible.

Another of Leber's achievements was the setting up of an endowment, in partnership with the employers, known as the *Stiftung Berufshilfe*, for the vocational training of orphans of trade unionists killed in an accident on a construction site. The attendance of the President of the Federal Republic at the formal ceremony to inaugurate the Foundation (significantly enough, it was held in the historic 'Paulskirche' in Frankfurt) was the first time in the country's history that a Head of State appeared at a predominantly trade union gathering; it was also the first time both evangelical and catholic churches were represented by bishops at a ceremony of this kind. Since then the churches have consistently been represented at the union's Congresses – a convincing proof how far the German trade union movement has come since its atheistic or, at least, decidedly anti-clerical days in the period up to 1914.

The last strike to occur in the industry (apart from a quite insignificant strike of tile fixers in 1967) took place in 1962. Both sides viewed it as a silly business and got together to ensure that disputes were settled in future in a less out-moded manner. The statement jointly issued shortly thereafter (known as the *Wiesbadener Empfehlungen*) indicates the spirit in which the industry's excellent industrial relations have been conducted ever since:

It will be the aim of the employers' federations and the union, each appreciating the functions and responsibilities of the other, to try and obtain the highest possible social level for the building industry based on the objective assessment of all relevant factors and economic possibilities open to the industry while at the same time paying due regard to the country's well-being.'

More will be said later in this chapter on the various matters agreed upon by the two sides for improving both the efficiency and the working conditions of the construction industry. An account of the achievements in this industry may help to counter an attitude to industrial relations that is leading some people despairingly to assume that strife and anarchy are the inevitable manifestations of some natural law; some, indeed, have gone so far as to formulate a doctrine of 'the balance of terror'. But, in passing, it is pleasant to refer to British industries – boot and shoes and some sections of the textile industries, for example – in which much the same painstaking effort, good-will, and close co-operation with employers has brought similar results. The British solution to disputes in the shoe industry was, in fact, arrived at much earlier than the German, the 'Terms of Settlement' agreed between the Federated Associations of Boot and Shoe Manufacturers and the National Union of Boot and Shoe Operatives going as far back as 1895; the proof of the sound commonsense of that settlement was provided by the 'National Conference Agreement' of February 1972 which merely restated and amplified the 1895 principles.

This is an example within Britain of the truth conspicuously demonstrated in West Germany (or in Austria, where the demonstration has been even more convincing) that it is possible to eradicate the conditions under which disputes become endemic once the absurdity of incessant industrial warfare in the second half of the twentieth century is recognised and union and employers set out to meet each other half-way – with, of course, the important proviso that trade union organisation and leadership is capable of keeping an inevitable minority of politically motivated trouble-makers at bay and, equally important, that the employers, for their part, have organised themselves efficiently.

Wage negotiations

Three years ago the two sides in the German construction industry decided to get their wage negotiations settled and done with, four months in advance of the expiry of the then current agreement, simply in order to give them time to prepare a joint case for an impending round of discussions with the Government on measures for further improving the industry's efficiency. This joint approach to the Government was aimed mainly at achieving a further extension and amplification of the regulations for 'bad weather working' introduced at the end of 1959 largely owing to the union's initiative. The following were the more important provisions in those regulations:

(1) The making available of grants or loans to private persons and non-governmental organisations willing to give contracts for building to be carried out or continued during the 'bad weather season', defined as 1st November to 31st March. Grants of up to 7.5% of gross wage costs could be made to qualified applicants for the erection of houses under the 'social building' programme and building programmes that qualified for tax rebate.

(2) Loans, or grants to meet interest on loans, were made available for building contractors for the purchase of plant and machinery, shelters and other protective equipment to enable building contracts to be carried out during the 'bad weather period'. The grants were aimed at meeting interest on amounts not exceeding DM1000 in respect of each worker required for a 'bad weather contract'.

(3) Building trade workers became eligible for the following payments:

  (i) Grants to those working away from home amounting to 50% of the cost of return fares for two journeys, a 40% grant being payable for a third journey home.
  (ii) Loans or grants up to a maximum of DM150 within a period of eighteen months for the purchase of additional essential protective clothing (working clothes and footwear).
  (iii) Separation allowances.

(4) Bad weather allowances (*Schlechtwettergeld*) were made payable without interrupting the contract of service on days when work could not be carried out owing to the weather. The payments were graduated according to family circumstances and were assessed at between 45% and 57% of gross earnings.

The success of these measures was soon demonstrated by a spectacular drop in the unemployment figures. Winter unemployment among construction workers had been running as high as 670,000 in 1957/1959 and over 600,000 in 1958/1959 but, following the passing of the 1959 law, unemployment came down to 239,000 in 1959/1960, 130,000 in 1960/1961 and to 43,000 in 1961/1962, thus setting a pattern that was pretty consistently followed right up to the recession of 1974.

But all this was merely the start. Three years later the grants or loans under (1) above had been raised to 11% of gross wage costs and various other adjustments and improvements in the scheme have since been made from time to time in the light of experience. Formerly, the payment of *Schlechtwettergeld* was restricted to the winter months. The outcome of the further approach by the two sides to the Government in 1972 resulted not only in some further easement of the qualifications for receiving *Schlechtwettergeld* but a noteworthy advance was made in that, for the first time, agreement was reached to pay, as from 1973, compensation for up to ten working hours lost through bad weather, outside the normal 'bad weather' period, i.e. even during the summer if bad weather conditions force work to stop. From 1974, the payment was extended to up to 24 lost working hours. It goes without saying that these schemes cost very large sums of money (much of it supplied by the Federal Labour Institute in Nürnberg) and, accordingly, the industry as a whole, and not only the union, occasionally comes in for criticism. It defends itself by pointing out that, when related to what has been achieved, the money has been well spent and the sums are small when compared with the financial losses associated with long drawn-out strikes. It might also be added that the union, when meeting the criticism that its policies have put up the price of housing, points out that building prices have gone up a great deal more in other countries that do not have to contend with anything like the same severity of winter working conditions as prevail over much of West Germany.

The union is understandably proud that it has achieved so much in an industry so notoriously difficult to organise. Of over 65,000 different firms only 10% are large enough to be regarded as industrial undertakings and, as such, organised by the Hauptverband der Deutschen Bauindustrie; the remainder come within the category '*Handwerk*' and are organised by the *Zentralverband des Deutschen Baugewerbes*. Although there are thus two employers' organisations there is only the one union, the Construction Workers', which is responsible for organising workers in all branches of the industry. The assertion too often made that 'industrial relations problems are inevitable on construction sites' finds no credence in West Germany and would be taken as an indication that employer and union were failing to carry out their jobs.

Union organisation

Clearly, a union such as the *Industriegewerkschaft Bau, Steine, Erden* can only fulfil its wide range of responsibilities by having an extremely efficient organisation, both at headquarters (in Frankfurt) and at 'Land' and district level. The union's Executive Committee has seven members in addition to the President and Vice-President and its regional organisation centres around ten focal points: Stuttgart, Munich, Frankfurt, Hannover, Hamburg, Düsseldorf, Bremen, Dortmund, Mainz and Berlin. It has an educational centre (the Jakob-Knöss-Haus) opened at Schwalbach in the Taunus in 1967, lavishly equipped with the latest teaching aids and ten holiday centres, three of them situated abroad – in France, Italy and

Austria. Incidentally, the running of such teaching and holiday centres is quite a feature of German trade unionism. The Metal Workers' Union has three educational centres and eight holiday centres, some of them able to bear comparison with hotels in the three or four-star category. The union also organises such special undertakings as the *Stiftung Berufshilfe* endowment already referred to, and has its special organisation for ensuring the smooth operation of the scheme for *Vermögensbildung* of which more will be said later. In common with other German unions it attaches great importance to its educational facilities, both for officials and for ordinary members, and it played a big part in the setting-up of the splendidly equipped vocational training centre at Simmerath.

The union pays special attention to its younger members and has had considerable success in keeping in touch with their needs and wishes. The leadership does not share the cynical view of the shepherd in *The Winter's Tale* –'Would that there were no age between sixteen and three-and-twenty, for there is nothing in the between but getting wenches with child, wronging the ancientry, stealing and fighting.' Union members up to the age of 'three-and-twenty' belong to a *Gemeinschaft Junger Gewerkschafter*. This actively concerns itself with forming various groups and committees which aim at keeping the following matters constantly under discussion:

(1) Present-day trade union problems;

(2) Problems of apprentices and safety precautions to be observed by young people on building sites;

(3) Participation in special courses run for trade union members, and

(4) Free-time activities.

In each of the union's administrative districts at least one representative of those in the age group up to 23 has to be elected and there is also a district sub-committee under the chairmanship of one of the younger members. Bored young men do not need to seek distraction in the forms of violence and extremism which certain left-wing youth organisations are ready to provide for them.

German trade unionism has never been organised on the cheap and members of the Construction Workers' Union are prepared to put a lot in, in order to get a lot out. The following table which sets out the membership dues operative in 1972 will enable a rough comparison to be made with the dues levied by British trade unions.

Stage	Gross weekly wage in DM	Fortnightly contribution in DM
1	155	6
2	170	6.50
3	190	7
4	210	8
5	250	9
6	280	10
7	310	11
8	340	12
9	370	13
10	430	15
11	500	18
12	600	24
13	700	30
14	800	45
15	over 800	60

'People's capitalism'

The union's leadership takes pride in asserting that the union does not use its power to exploit the bargaining situation of key groups of workers at the expense of the old, the poor and the low paid. Not being in conflict with the capitalist system, it has had no hesitation in continuing to follow the tradition built up over the last twelve years of assisting the workers, with the backing of employers, to build up their capital assets. More will be said about this in a subsequent chapter. All that need be said here is that it was this union that pioneered the idea of 'people's capitalism', using such slogans as 'ownership for all in a free society' and 'without property there can be no freedom', with such vigour and success that it induced the Government to pass the original '312 DM Law' of 1961 which, after some interim revisions, was expanded into the 'DM624 Law' of June 1970. Although the dictum that 'Money is like muck, not good except it be spread, is as old as Francis Bacon, its sensible, if limited, acceptance in the Federal Republic owes much to the union that has done so much to demonstrate how much more can be obtained for the workers by constructive planning and co-operation than by militancy.

There are, of course, some lowering clouds on the horizon. In common with other unions, the Construction Workers' Union is finding that it has to contend today with a great deal more skilfully organised activity on the part of politically-motivated extremists than ever before. But the leadership and union officials are standing firm and pressing on with their efforts to keep improving the working conditions and standards of living of the membership — in other words, in giving effect to one of the union's slogans: *Für eine humane Arbeitswelt* ('We want a humane working world').

9

Co-determination: background and practical application

It is customary to give the word *Mitbestimmung* its literal translation, 'co-determination' but, in plain English, it simply means 'workers participation in management'. The conception of co-determination has unfortunately become so complicated and controversial that it is tempting to regard it as a peculiarly German issue, best left as a preoccupation for German experts – particularly when, as has sometimes happened, the tangled skein is no sooner unravelled than it seems to get itself into a greater tangle than before.

The conceptions of 'workers participation'

Its intricacies, however, become much less complex once a clear distinction is drawn between the two competing conceptions of 'workers participation' that have long jostled one another for pride of place in West Germany: i.e. one-third participation as opposed to fifty-fifty (parity) participation. Moreover, an issue so intimately associated with the German trade union movement and to which it attaches paramount importance is not to be lightly passed over. Again, it would be unfortunate if the complexities with which it has become associated were to divert attention from some of the simple and very effective procedures it has evolved – procedures that, after suitable modification, may well be adopted by British industry.

It so happens that the theme of *Mitbestimmung* has the unenviable reputation of having been more written about than almost any other subject in the socio-political field. Between the first succinct enunciation of the doctrine in 1928 by Naphtali in his work *Wirtschaftsdemokratie, ihr Wesen, Weg and Ziel* and the year 1961, an expert who had been carefully listing the number of publications issued on the subject, announced that by then it had reached 9,633. That number must since have quadrupled and there is no sign that the output is decreasing. Even in Germany, inclined by tradition to display kindly tolerance for 'sophistical rhetoricians', the incessant output month by month of all shapes and sizes of publications ranging from the expensive tome to the cheap paper-back, some of them theoretical in the extreme, has come to be regarded with something akin to consternation and awe.

Not only has *Mitbestimmung* in general and *paritätische' Mitbestimmung* (i.e. fifty-fifty workers' participation with management) in particular held the German Trade Union Federation under its sway. Many others, perhaps unaware of it themselves, have 'dwelt so long upon the thought that it has taken them prisoner'. It has, for example, exercised a remarkable attraction over German universities and the churches. Both the encyclical *Quadragesimo Anno* and its successor *Mater et Magistra* show traces of Naphtali's ideas and, although none of his colleagues is likely to match the output of the Jesuit Professor Oswald von Nell-Breuning, several prominent ecclesiastical pedagogues have given the impression that they are interested more in *Mitbestimmung* than in theology.

In addition, various well-endowed institutions, with large staffs of diligent back-room boys, like the 'Hans-Böckler-*Gesellschaft*' and the *Stiftung Mitbestimmung* (both formed in 1954), have made it their business to see that interest, or at all events uneasy attention, is never allowed to flag. They are very well-informed people quietly pursuing their aim of achieving what they have convinced themselves is a proper share of economic power. A British observer, little given to philosophical disquisition and accustomed to more empirical and pragmatic methods of approach, may be inclined to flinch away from so much earnestness and become embarrassed and ill-at-ease as he contemplates such undeviating tenacity of purpose. But the trade unions, so ably abetted by the publicists, have held doggedly to their course and German industrialists have been given no option but to take very seriously indeed proposals for *paritätische Mitbestimmung* which, they are convinced (rightly or wrongly) would hamstring their enterprises and impair their competitive efficiency. No politician dares stand aside from a controversy which has raged inside and outside the Bundestag with varying degrees of intensity for over twenty-five years.

Historical background

Leaving aside for a moment the heated controversies of recent years, a brief historical description has to be attempted of the legislation that was operative during the period 1951 to 1971. Three principal Acts and two different types of co-determination are involved:

(1) A law enacted in 1951 to provide for co-determination in the iron and steel and coal mining industries. This law, the *Mitbestimmungsgesetz*, is still operative and uncompromisingly applies *paritätische* or parity *Mitbestimmung* in a closely defined field.

(2) A law, originally enacted in 1952, covering private employment in general and known as the Works Constitution Act (*Betriebsverfassungsgesetz*), which was much amended and amplified on 1st January 1972.

(3) A law, originally enacted in 1955, applying, in effect, the *Betriebsverfassungsgesetz* to the field of public employment. This is known as the *Personalvertretungsgesetz* – the Act on Staff Councils in the Public Services.

There are wide differences in conception and scope between the 1951 law and the laws of 1952 and 1955. The 1951 law is the 'real thing' in the eyes of the adherents of *paritätische Mitbestimmung* and very thoroughly applies the concept to the two industries with which it is concerned. Its origins go back to the days of British Military Government when an agreement was made with the trade unions providing, *inter alia*, for the establishment in the British Zone of Supervisory Boards (*Aufsichtsräte*) in the coal and steel industries, consisting of an equal number of representatives of employers and employees, and the appointment by the unions of a Labour Director (*Arbeitsdirektor*) who would also become a member of the firm's Executive Board (*Vorstand*). In 1949 one of the first demands made by the unions on the newly created Federal Government in Bonn had been to give this form of co-determination in the coal and steel industries legislative backing; the unions under Böckler's leadership were intent at that time on accomplishing, as they put it, 'the economic emancipation of the workers as the complement to their political emancipation'. While management accepted the workers' demand for co-determination in the personnel and social field it rejected the demand for co-determination in economic decisons; it regarded this as an infringement of the system of free enterprise which, as employers saw it, was the only way by which Germany could be rebuilt. Before the Bundestag could discuss a government bill on co-determination, the unions threatened to strike and the Government promptly gave in.

The bill which became law shortly afterwards (relating, it must be emphasised once again, only to the steel and coal mining industries) was a major triumph for the unions. Its main provisions were briefly as follows:

(1) The Supervisory Board (*Aufsichtsrat*) of an enterprise covered by the Law is to consist of eleven members: four to represent shareholders,

plus one additional member; four to represent employees and trade unions, plus an extra member; an eleventh, neutral, member has also to be appointed.

(2) A Labour Director (*Arbeitsdirektor*) must be appointed as a member of equal standing with the other members of the Executive Board (*Vorstand*). He is responsible for social and personnel problems, and his election and recall is, in effect, in the hands of the unions.

To turn now to the second law – the Works Constitution Act or *Betriebsverfassungsgesetz* of 1952 – this differed fundamentally from the law of 1951 by presenting a much watered-down version of co-determination. The writer would suggest that it is this milder form of *Mitbestimmung* that merits careful study in Britain rather than *paritätische Mitbestimmung* – something that seems impossible of reconciliation with British company law. This 1952 law might well be regarded as having done as much as any other single factor to contribute to Germany's remarkable post-war record of peaceful industrial relations. The spirit that underlies it is shown in the following clause:

'The employer and the works council shall work together in a spirit of mutual trust under the applicable collective agreements in co-operation with the trade unions and employers' associations represented in the undertaking, for the good of the undertaking and its employees, having due regard to the interests of the community'.

It was nevertheless a great disappointment to the unions. Among other things they were disturbed to find that the more limited rights of co-determination which it prescribed were related not specifically to trade unions but to firms' workers and employees; the 1951 law, by contrast, provided for far-reaching co-determination functions to be exercised specifically by trade unions.

Of the third law – the Act on Staff Councils in the Public Services (the *Personalvertretungsgesetz*) of 1955 – it is only necessary to say that it extended the provisions of the law of 1952 to the field of public employment. It was replaced on 15th March 1974 by a revised *Bundespersonalvertretungsgesetz* that brought up-to-date and redefined many of the detailed provisions of the original law; the aim was to extend the rights of public servants to co-determination (*Mitbestimmung*) as well as to consultation or co-operation (*Mitwirkung*) in their places of work. The scope for co-determination given to public service employees is necessarily more narrowly defined and restricted than in the field of private industry.

The implementation of the 1952 Law was mandatory on employers and their employees and covered all privately owned firms in the Federal

Republic. Only small enterprises with less than five permanently employed persons (or less than ten in agriculture and forestry) were exempted from the law. The Act required the following bodies to be set up:

(1) *The Works Council (Betriebsrat).* This affords representation of the firm's personnel in due legal form. It is elected secretly and directly by all the firm's personnel entitled to vote. It serves for a two-year term. If an enterprise consists of several plants, and if the individual works councils so wish, they may set up a joint works council.

(2) *The Works Assembly (Betriebsversammlung).* This mass meeting includes all employees. The chairman of the works council presides. It may discuss matters of direct concern to the firm and to the personnel but it has to leave to employers' organisations and trade unions such wider issues as collective bargaining.

(3) *The Economic Committee (Wirtschaftsausschuss).* This group is established in firms with more than 100 persons permanently on the pay-roll. Its tasks are to promote co-operation between the works council and the employer and to encourage information on economic matters. In a way it is both an educational group, serving the interests of better informing management and staff, and a liaison body. It has from four to eight members, half of them appointed by management and half by the works council.

(4) *The Supervisory Board (Aufsichtstrat)* of joint stock companies has to be composed one-third of representatives of employees. These representatives are elected directly by all personnel entitled to vote.

The essential provisions set out above were retained and elaborated in a revised Works Constitution Act *(Betriebsverfassungsgesetz)* that went through Parliament at the end of 1971. This provides a degree of *Mitbestimmung* still falling far short of the unions' demands for *paritätische* or *qualifizierte Mitbestimmung.* The bill's difficult passage through Parliament will be referred to later in some detail because the controversies it engendered threw into sharp relief the essential differences between ordinary *Mitbestimmung* (one-third worker participation in management) and *paritätische Mitbestimmung* (fifty-fifty worker participation in management). Before dealing with these controversies, however, it is necessary to have another look at the historical background.

Works Council Law

The conception of worker participation in management was given its first practical application by the Works Council Law as far back as 1920. This provided a measure of workers' representation throughout private enterprise: every firm employing more than a certain number of workers had to form a works council. A 1922 amendment to the Law went further by providing for the election of two workers' representatives to the Supervisory Board (*Aufsichtsrat*) of joint stock companies, thus giving the workers a certain measure of insight into, and influence on, the overall policy of the firm. Works councils were swept away by Hitler in 1933 but re-established by Military Government under Control Council Law No. 22 of 1946 and confirmed, more or less in their present form, by the Works Constitution Act of 1952. Works councils have thus a long and successful history behind them.

Paritätische Mitbestimmung, or to use the often used but, for an English reader, not very happily worded phrase *qualifizierte Mitbestimmung* (which almost lends itself to the translation: 'unqualified co-determination'!), is regarded in some quarters as tantamount to a claim on behalf of organised labour to share in the control of the economy. There has always been a demand for this on the part of the DGB and its constituent unions but it is only during the last six or seven years that it has been pressed with such energy as to be constantly in the forefront as a major political issue. The DGB's continued insistence on parity co-determination has indeed been an incessant embarrassment to the two coalition parties, the Social Democrats (SPD) and the Free Democrats (FDP), ever since they formed their Government; it continued to be so even after the passing of the second Works Constitution Act of 1971 and has more than once threatened to drive a wedge between the two parties. (Even the impetuous passing of yet another Works Constitution Law in the Parliamentary Session preceding the elections of Autumn 1976 may have won only a temporary respite as the DGB remain dissatisfied. But that is looking ahead to a matter proper to a later chapter.)

Workers' control

'Workers' control' is, of course, a concept to which syndicalist and guild syndicalist ideas have inevitably made their contribution; its attraction is irresistible to left-wing militants convinced that conflict between capital and labour is fundamental and irreconcilable. German trade union theoreticians, despite the not inconsiderable contribution they have themselves made to the enormous literature on the topic, do not appear to have been unduly influenced by the syndicalists and are to be acquitted of any intention of using the concept of 'workers power' as a means of overthrowing the present democratic order – they have never for a moment regarded workers' control as a substitute for democracy. Their argument is, rather, that it is in the interests of preserving, whilst simultaneously bettering, the existing order that the 'undue power of management' must be curbed by fifty-fifty trade union participation in every aspect of managerial activity. The DGB (itself something of a capitalist undertaking, though showing nothing of the 'ugly face' thereof) is a stalwart upholder of the Federal Republic's system of political democracy and, as already mentioned, free from the sinister motives associated with 'workers power' even if its demands go so far that the German Employers' Confederation (BDA) has alleged that the aim is to 'create a network of centrally steered trade union control over the entire economy, thus constituting an unprecedented amalgamation of power in the hands of the trade union movement'.

The Biedenkopf Report

The Social-Democratic Party has never worked up as much enthusiasm for *paritätische Mitbestimmung* as the DGB would like and the Opposition, the conservative Christian Democratic Party (CDU/CSU), with the very important exception of a minority group within it about which more will be said later, even less; the SPD's Coalition partners, the Free Democrats were vigorously opposed to the idea from the very outset. When the campaign for parity *Mitbestimmung* first began to work up, Parliament, with a view to getting the issue out of the political arena, at least for the time being, had recourse, at the end of 1967, to the traditional delaying device of referring the matter to a Commission. This consisted of nine professors, chaired by a Dr. Biedenkopf who was subsequently to play a political role of ever-increasing importance.

The Commission's report was not submitted until January 1970 but it proved, on examination, to be a thoroughly practical and workmanlike document. The Commission accepted the concept that 'management's job is to manage' and, after taking a good look at the operation of *paritätische Mitbestimmung* in the two industries, steel and coal, in which it already operates, made clear its view that a Supervisory Board (*Aufsichtsrat*) cannot function effectively unless it can be sure of a clear majority. Nevertheless, the Commission placed the fullest possible weight on the need for workers to be given a proper say in decision-making and on the importance of involving them in the way a firm is run; after all, as the report very properly stressed, their jobs may be at stake. On the other hand, it also emphasised that due weight must be given to shareholders' interests and attention was drawn to the risk that undertakings may well lose their driving force and initiative if obliged constantly to compromise between the competing attitudes of divergent interests. In short, Biedenkopf decided on a 7:5 ratio in favour of the shareholders and firmly rejected *Parität*.

The report came as a blow to the DGB. Its first reaction, however, was one of good sense and moderation; it announced that, although *paritätische Mitbestimmung* would always remain its ultimate aim, it was prepared, as a first step, to accept Biedenkopf's suggestions for an improvement of the Works Constitution Law of 1952. This sensible statement immediately eased the tension. Unfortunately, however, it was not long before a document was found circulating in Parliamentary circles which reflected most of the DGB's well-known ideas and which, indeed, was in essence a re-hash of detailed proposals which the DGB had unsuccessfully put forward some two years earlier in the hope of getting them accepted by the Social Democratic Party. The Employers' Confederation was incensed when the existence of the draft came to its notice and a marked estrangement followed between BDA and DGB at a time when their common fear of left-wing activists had been drawing them closer together.

Before the present Minister of Labour and Social Affairs, Herr Walter Arendt, took office on the formation of the first SPD/FDP Coalition Government in 1969, he had been head of the Mineworkers' Union. In that capacity he had had a great deal to do with the system of *paritätische Mitbestimmung* existing in the coal industry for the last twenty years and it was inevitable that he should be attracted by the DGB's proposals. He accordingly arranged for the preparation of a draft bill – often known as the 'Arendt draft' – which, although it stopped just short of equal participation, went a long way in many respects to meet the DGB's most cherished aims and hopes. This draft was circulated in October 1970. It got a favourable response from the unions but came in for angry denunciation from other quarters. The attitude of the Free Democrats, the coalition partners of the Social Democrats, stiffened still further; they made it very clear that they were not going to be associated with anything that might assist the cause of *paritätische Mitbestimmung*. The outcome of six weeks of feverish activity, much of it behind closed doors, was the presentation by the Minister on 3rd December 1970 of a revised draft which, he announced, had received Cabinet approval.

A revised Works Constitution Bill

The new draft bill (the *Regierungsentwurf*) showed few points of resemblance with its predecessor. There was a marked change of emphasis. It was no longer a bill providing the DGB with a bridge-head for the ultimate achievement of *paritätische Mitbestimmung* but, in its new form, exactly what it purported to be: an improved version of the well-tried Works Constitution Law (*Betriebsverfassungsgesetz*) of 1952.

The unions were taken aback. The DGB described the new version as 'alarming' and pilloried the Free Democrats as directly responsible for the change of front (as indeed, they may well have been). It can hardly have been taken by surprise at their attitude, however; far more vexatious was what it regarded as the 'sell-out' on the part of the Social-Democratic Party, from which it had hoped for better things. The DGB was on the horns of a dilemma: should it bring fresh pressure to bear on its friends in the Social-Democratic Party or renounce a large part of its wishes? Having fought so long and so devotedly for the cause, it was humiliating to have to retreat when victory had seemed so near. It knew, however, that if matters were pressed too far, the Social Democrats might get embroiled with the Free Democrats and imperil the Coalition – and this was the last thing it wished to see happen.

The unions' embarrassment was the greater as they must have been conscious that a large part of their membership was, at best, lukewarm. Sooner or later there comes a stage when every trade union movement has to assess how far its membership is prepared to support it on an outstanding point of principle – and on the *Mitbestimmung* issue shop-floor views make a fascinating subject for study. Despite basic similarities of view between trade unionists the world over, divergent trends are becoming increasingly apparent between one country and another in the matter of class-consciousness and the 'cloth-cap' image. Although British trade unionists are sometimes surprised to find that their German counterparts may have a university degree, the time is long since past when a trade union leader in the Federal Republic was regarded with suspicion and distrust on account of his good academic qualifications; he is not thereby dismissed as an 'intellectual', with the implication that he is a useless theorist. On the contrary, if he is rather better educated than most of the union members so much the better; they expect him to have a wider experience and broader vision than is to be acquired on the shop floor. Nevertheless their leadership's devotion to the conception of *paritätische Mitbestimmung* sometimes puzzles them and this lack of enthusiasm on the part of the membership was brought into the open by the decidedly half-hearted backing given to many of the *Mitbestimmung* rallies on which the DGB had set such high hopes during 1970. There can be little doubt that the average worker finds the whole thing rather above his head and has little taste for a controversy that sometimes gives rise to metaphysical flights of fancy and doctrinal quirks repugnant to his commonsense. He is conscious that, having regard to the achievements of German industry in recent years, there cannot really be much wrong with a management that has attained for the Federal Republic, starting from scratch, a degree of industrial prosperity seldom matched and never surpassed. Moreover, with understandable modesty, he feels that he is, in the last resort, better equipped to play his part on the shop floor than in the

Board room. He is reasonably well satisfied with the operation of the existing works councils but when the question at issue is that of fifty–fifty *paritätische Mitbestimmung* the average German worker does not merely give little thought to it; he does not even think he ought to give much thought to it.

A perceptive union leadership

But if such is the somewhat unenthusiastic attitude of a large part of the membership – an attitude which the trade union leadership is reluctant to admit but which seemed to be confirmed by the results of an inquiry undertaken by the Institut für Demoskopie in 1974 – the fullest weight must be given to the sincerity and intense conviction of that leadership. It would be less than fair at this point to refrain from mentioning how fortunate West Germany has been since 1945 in having union leaders with perceptive insight into managerial problems, men who have thrown their whole weight behind management in steadily expanding, by every method available, the output of goods and thereby creating more and more real wealth. That the German worker has never lost sight of the simple truth that it is higher industrial production that creates the wealth that makes payment of higher wages possible, is due in large measure to the way the leadership has drilled this lesson home. It is this interest in the prosperity and expansion of industry that has led the bigger unions, under the leadership of exceptionally able men, to build up a remarkable cadre of very well qualified persons in every way competent to play a distinguished part on management boards; there is every justification for the confidence of the trade union leadership in its ability and competence to share the tasks of management. It is indeed this very confidence in their competence that has led these leaders to press their claim for *paritätische Mitbestimmung* with an embarrassing pertinacity that sometimes frightens those who might otherwise be their allies. It is also necessary to emphasise that there are very special reasons to explain and justify the DGB's crusading zeal. The German trade union movement cannot forget that an important factor in the collapse of the Weimar Republic was the concentration of economic power in the hands of a very few men – men who, by financing the National Socialist movement helped Hitler to destroy German democracy and, with it, any real and effective trade unionism for twelve long painful years. The men who followed Böckler have, like him, never flinched in their determination to prevent another dictatorship, whether of the right or of the left. So, while German trade unionists share with their British colleagues a lively recollection of the suffering associated with widespread unemployment they have other still more painful memories: runaway inflation, communist intrigue and fascist dictatorship. It is hardly surprising that they are convinced that parity co-determination affords the best means of combating such dangers.

The passing of the Works Constitution Act 1971

There were nevertheless many who thought it unwise for the unions to break another lance for parity *Mitbestimmung* at this particular juncture. But their hopes had been raised high by the appearance of the 'Arendt' draft and they began looking around for fresh allies. This seems to explain a most remarkable decision by the DGB early in 1971 to appeal direct to the parliamentary opposition, the Christian Democratic party, just before that party held its Congress, for aid 'in giving reality to trade union wishes for greater participation in management'. It shows how many wheels within wheels there are on this issue! That the Christian Democratic Party (in effect the Conservative opposition to the present SPD/FDP Coalition Government) should thus have been approached is due to the important role played within it by a minority group (the Sozialausschüsse) under the leadership of a former Minister of Labour and Social Affairs, Hans Katzer. The views of this formidable social reformer were known to be further to the left than those of many Social Democrats. Whatever his political motives may have been – there was the inevitable, if unfair, criticism that he was seeking to enhance his own prestige and that of his party by 'dishing the Social Democrats' – no one could call in question the sincerity of his desire for social reform; moreover, his views had considerable appeal for young people within the party's 'Junge Union'.

There were many in his Party, however, who by no means shared Herr Katzer's views and had been deriving solace, comfort and conviction from the professorial distate for *Parität* expressed in the Biedenkopf report. But as the Party Congress had had placed before it four different *Mitbestimmung* proposals, there seemed a remote chance that Katzer's eloquence might win over some bewildered waverers and, with the vote of the Junge Union, even get backing for *paritätische Mitbestimmung* – in this instance, what is known as the '4:2:4 model'. The Conservative Opposition would then have been able to put forward proposals much closer to trade union wishes than the Government's bill! In the event, however, Katzer's proposals were backed by only 111 of the 530 delegates present; the Junge Union had been working away at a formula of its own (6:2:4) and was evidently not to be enticed away from it. Biedenkopf himself was present and pressed his views with such ability that it became evident that the *Arbeitgeberflügel*, the business interests, were bound to win. With Katzer defeated, the Congress decided, by a close vote of 259 to 253, to adopt the '6:4:2 model' (i.e. 6 shareholders: 4 workers: 2 co-opted members) – something not far away from the original Biedenkopf proposals. Having put Katzer and his colleagues to rout, the Party sought to close its ranks and make some semblance of advancing as a united phalanx to do battle with the Government. Those on the Party's left wing, however, were so obviously marching unarmed that it was clear to all that the Government's bill was not going to be imperilled by any sudden adventurous sally on the part of the Opposition. The Government was not going to be 'dished' and the bill's passage through the Bundestag was henceforth assured. The new *Betriebsverfassungsgesetz* duly became law at the end of the year.

10

The Works Constitution Act of 1971

Although extremely disappointed at the introduction of the Works Constitution Act, the DGB could not but admit that, even if what in their view was the 'best' had been pushed to one side, the Act nevertheless made many improvements to the old *Betriebsverfassungsgesetz* which were very well worth having. Indeed, it was hardly to be disputed that the Works Constitution Law in its revised form had eradicated almost every minor weakness brought to light during the previous Law's twenty years of practical operation. The vital role of works councils had been emphatically re-affirmed – a role that has given workers a sense of 'belonging' to the firm which employs them and has done much to eradicate the 'us' versus 'them' attitude. By providing a means for ensuring that grievances are dealt with promptly and not allowed to fester, works councils have taken away from shop-floor militants a great many opportunities for stirring up trouble and have done much to ameliorate the atmosphere of mutual distrust and suspicion that tends from time to time to pervade certain industries.

The working of the Act

In the nature of things, any compromise, such as the 1971 Law undoubtedly is, between the views and aims of conflicting interests leaves theoreticians and perfectionists disillusioned and dissatisfied. Many employers as well as trade unions were disappointed that their views were not given greater expression. Although the DGB had not abated one jot of its demands for fifty–fifty co-partnership individual unions were soon displaying their good sense by quietly pointing to the good points of the new legislation. Inevitably there were employers who complained that unreasonable inroads had been made on managerial responsibilities – complaints, however, that were soon muted. The law has certainly given workers a greater say in day-to-day matters affecting their working lives and their prospects of continued employment but it would be difficult to maintain that managerial responsibilities have been eroded to the extent some employers were at first inclined to allege. Managers have not, for example, been deprived of the right to manage their undertakings in the way they see fit even though the new Law has undoubtedly strengthened the authority of the works councils in matters of personnel management; it is only in this limited sense that 'inroads' can be said to have been made on what once used to be regarded as a field of managerial prerogative. Works councils have at last been given a say where new jobs are concerned and may, if they see fit, ensure that new jobs are offered in the first place to workers already in the employ of the firm. They are also given a big say in questions affecting working processes and the environment in which the work is carried out. For the first time the rights of the individual worker are set out in statutory form; he now has the right to examine the file kept on him by the personnel department and any observations he cares to make on the information contained therein will have to be put on that file. And, although foreign workers previously had the right to vote in works council elections, the 1971 Law for the first time made them eligible for election – an important factor at a time when well over two million foreign workers were already employed in West Germany.

All the previous rights of works councils were not only confirmed by the 1971 Law but more closely defined in respect of such matters as the fixing of working hours; the drawing up of general leave arrangements; the use of technical devices controlling the quality of workmanship; the availability and allocation of flats and houses; the setting-up and nature of social facilities; the practical application of piece-work rates and bonuses. Previously, works councils had merely been consulted in respect of individual dismissals or engagements; from January 1972 they have had to be consulted when organisational changes are made.

Right at the outset, under the heading 'Status of trade unions and employers' associations', Part 1 of the 1971 Law makes the following statement (thus repeating in part the wording of the Law of 1952):

(1) The employer and the works council shall work together in a spirit of mutual trust having regard to the applicable collective agreements and in co-operation with the trade unions and employers' associations represented in the undertaking, for the good of the employees and of the undertaking.

(2) With a view to permitting the trade unions represented in the undertaking to exercise the power and duties laid down by the Act, their agents shall, after notifying the employer or his representative, be granted access to the undertaking, in so far as this does not run

counter to essential operational requirements, mandatory safety rules or the protection of trade secrets.

(3) This Act shall not affect the functions of trade unions and employers' associations and more particularly the protection of their members' interests.

A particular important part of the Act has to do with the setting up of Finance (Economic) Committees. The relevant sections read as follows:

(1) 'In all enterprises having normally more than 100 permanent employees a Finance Committee must be set up. This Committee is charged with the duty of conferring with the employer on financial matters and informing the works council accordingly.'

(2) 'The employer is obliged to keep the Finance Committee fully and regularly informed of the financial affairs of the undertaking by providing the necessary documentation in so far as the production and business secrets of the enterprise are not thereby endangered, and also to set out the implications for personnel planning.'

(3) 'Financial affairs within the meaning of (2) include:

   (i) The economic and financial position of the company;
   (ii) The production and marketing situation;
   (iii) The production and investment programme;
   (iv) Rationalisation plans;
   (v) Production techniques and working methods, especially the introduction of new working methods.
   (vi) The reduction of operations within the works, or closure of works or parts of works.
   (vii) Change of location of works or parts of works.
   (viii) Fusion of companies.
   (ix) Changes in the works organisation or in the objectives of the company, and
   (x) Any other matters which could fundamentally affect the interests of the employees of the enterprise.

The Finance Committee shall consist of at least three, but not more than seven, members who must be employees of the Company and at least one shall be a works council member. . . . The Committee members must have the technical and personal qualifications required for the carrying-out of their duties.'

All this represents an appreciable stiffening-up of the former requirements concerning Finance (or Economic) Committees. The old sub-section was more woolly. Instead of the wording 'in order to promote co-operation in a spirit of confidence, etc.' the new section comes straight to the point and charges the Finance Committee with specific duties. The new sub-section (3) above has also spelt things out in a good deal more detail, i.e. (v), (vi), (vii), (viii), and (ix) are significant new requirements.

The Conciliation Board

What, however, gave rise to more anxiety on the employer's side was a new provision that a works council would in future have behind it an '*Einigungsstelle*', or conciliation board, to which matters in dispute could be referred; provision was made for equal representation of employers and employees with a neutral chairman (with casting vote) presiding. Management feared that it might be outvoted on matters intimately affecting the future of the undertaking, e.g. a merger or closure, but, as the '*Einigungsstelle*' is legally required to give full weight to the firm's interests, this fear does not seem in practice to have been justified. Incidentally, either the employer or the works council may make an appeal to a Labour Court if the conciliation board is thought to have exceeded its powers.

The Act in operation

To sum up, although the Act of 1971 has only been in operation for not much more than three years it already seems to have justified itself as an admirable piece of legislation. It has unquestionably played its part in many undertakings in helping to nip grievances in the bud. Whether its provisions can always eradicate the bitterness so easily aroused whenever large-scale redundancies arise has not perhaps been put to a really conclusive test, but workers these days can hardly assert that they have been inadequately consulted or have been ridden over roughshod by their employer; it is only high-handed ruthless management that has cause to object to the Act's new provisions, not the enlightened employer. Workers, in short, have now been identified more closely than ever with their firm and their industry. Although no one would be so rash as to maintain, having regard to the whole host of historical, economic and organisational factors involved, that an Act of this kind could be transferred to Britain lock, stock and barrel, it nevertheless points the way to methods whereby more effective participation could be introduced into British industries without thereby discouraging initiative. Participation is not something to be offered by a tired management to its workers as a desperate last resort after interminable industrial warfare; the 1971 Act embodies fifty years of practical experience and as such merits the most painstaking study.

11

The Works Constitution Act of 1976

The passing of the 1971 Works Constitution Act, with provisions that came into effect on 1st January immediately following, might well have been thought a suitable opportunity for the protagonists of *Mitebestimmung* to relax, regain their breath and enjoy a well-earned respite before undertaking the next campaign. Not so! The printers ink was hardly dry before the embarrassed Coalition Government found itself once more under heavy pressure to pass legislation to bring full *paritätische Mitbestimmung* into effect. The DGB would perhaps be reluctant to subscribe to the truth that legislative enactments, like men, may sometimes be 'moulded out of faults, and for the most, become much more the better for being a little bad' even though it is certainly true that the German unions, with their tradition of independence, are not generally inclined to regard legislation as a sort of universal or sole panacea.

But the DGB regarded the new law as simply not good enough and it was not long before the Coalition partners found themselves having to take some steps in the direction of parity co-determination; they therefore set about formulating proposals that they vainly hoped would prove acceptable to a wide range of interests.

The drive towards parity participation

Few would ever have envisaged the Social Democrat and Free Democrat party parliamentary groups coming together to reach an agreement under certain broad headings to bring about worker participation in management on a parity basis. After much wrangling, however, they were doing just that – and linking it up with certain proposals for stimulating capital accumulation in the hands of the workers. All along there was much opposition on the part of the Christian Democrats and progress soon began to be held up by some awkward new complications, hitherto only dimly suspected, arising out of proposals for providing for a third group of employees known as *leitende Angestellte*, i.e. those in positions of greater authority than people in the other two groups comprising *Arbeiter* (unskilled or semi-skilled workers for the most part) and *Angestellte* (white-collar workers). Other complications, almost too numerous to attempt to enumerate, then arose including some subtle complexities in respect of company law and the position of foreign-owned undertakings.

It was, however, the introduction of the new group of *leitende Angestellte* in the Government's draft bill that made havoc of all the previous ratios. The good old days when such simple ratios as 4:2:4 or 6:2:4 or 6:4:2 could be juggled with were past and gone. The ratios now coming under consideration began to give rise to tricky permutations calling for mathematical ability of almost the same high order as is required of those who seek to understand the theories of the ingenious Professor d'Hondt as applied to the German electoral system.

Still worse was to come. Every organisation interested in *Mitbestimmung* hastened to submit its own peculiar scheme and those debating the Government's proposals found themselves confronted with no fewer than fifteen alternative versions, as follows:

> The SPD 'model', with variants I, II and III; the FDP 'model', with variants I and II, the CDU 'model'; the model of the CDU Sozialausschüsse; the model of the CDU *Junge Union*; the DGB model; the DAG model; the EKD model (the version submitted by the Evangelical Church); the BKU model (the version of the Catholic employers) and the KAB model (the version of the Catholic workers movement).

Then came a further development that led some German industrial correspondents to speak of the final 'Waterloo for *paritätische Mitbestimmung*'. This was the appearance in October 1974 of the findings of two learned Professors who had been charged with the task of making a detailed analysis of the latest proposals. One was the Berlin constitutional lawyer, Scholz; the other, an expert from Giessen university, Raiser. Many of the conclusions reached by Professor Scholz, in his *'Gutachten'* of two hundred pages, tallied fairly closely with those of his colleague Raiser; significantly enough the view was expressed that *Parität* might well in actual practice mean *Überparität*, i.e. something more than 'parity' on the part of the workers. What was really disturbing was that both professors shared similar doubts as to whether the Government's bill was reconcilable with the Basic Law (Grundgesetz). This in itself seemed to make it pretty clear that the bill would never emerge from the Committee stage.

It is hardly surprising that during much of 1975 the conviction was steadily growing that, in view of the bewildering varieties and complexities, to say nothing of legal subtleties, presented by the many forms of *paritätische Mitbestimmung* jostling one another for consideration, the Coalition Government would be well advised to let the issue slip out of sight as quietly and unobtrusively as possible, the more so as some of the protagonists (though not, of course, the DGB) both within and without the Bundestag were showing signs of weariness; to 'keep up with the Jones's' on a matter of such intricacy was demanding wellnigh superhuman endurance on the part of parliamentarians, trade unionists (the DAG, for example), employers' organisations, theologians and theoreticians of every political colour.

Though very few would have expected it, a parliamentary miracle was, however, just round the corner. The Federal Chancellor, Helmut Schmidt, had no sooner taken office than he made it clear that he was not going to allow ideology to divert him from the realm of the possible and his policy of fair-minded commonsense soon began to win for him the trust and support of both sides of industry. The industrialists naturally tended at first to be somewhat on their guard before reposing increasing confidence in him, but, from the outset, the Chancellor's relations with the unions were extremely close. This close contact was not without its disadvantages as the unions clearly deserved, and expected, some acknowledgement from the Government of the public spirit they had manifested in exercising such a remarkable degree of wage restraint. Even before he succeeded Herr Willy Brandt as Chancellor, Herr Schmidt had several times had occasion to praise the unions for holding back; in 1972 and 1973, for example, they had demanded wage increases of no more that 7%–8% at a time when British unions were pressing for 35% – 40%. It was hardly possible at this stage, despite the misgivings of the constitutional lawyers and the many other difficulties in the way, to ignore their continuing determination to obtain fifty–fifty co-determination. The Chancellor thus attended the DGB's Hamburg Congress in May 1975 in the knowledge that some affirmative statement would be expected of him.

The Chancellor's views on parity

The first part of his speech was a review of the economic situation, in which he paid his usual warm tribute to the part the German trade union movement had played in enabling the Federal Republic to deal so much more successfully with the problem of world-inflation than almost any other country. He acknowledged that without the co-operation of the trade unions 'we should not now be living in comprehensive social, economic and, above all, political stability'. If the unions had not taken the responsible attitude that they had – an 'attitude orientated to the common good' – the Federal Republic would not at that moment be enjoying its present standing in the world.

When he came to the question of parity co-determination, he tackled this with no attempt at evasion. He was well aware, he said, that there were a number of delegates in the hall who would rather go without a law altogether than be presented with one that fell short of their full demands. As realists, however – and politicians, like trade unionists, must be realists – two things had to be kept in mind. If they were to reject in principle the measure of co-determination that could still be obtained during the lifetime of the present Parliament they would be playing straight into the hands of those who rejected co-determination altogether. If co-determination was to be dropped as an issue now, so favourable an opportunity to achieve worker participation might never recur.

In saying this, the Chancellor must have been well aware of the unusual degree of support he was beginning to receive from many divergent quarters. He was plainly hinting that the Government would not be able to go quite as far as the DGB would wish; nevertheless, he was evidently convinced that some further step towards parity co-determination was still possible. By getting the trade unions on his side he would be in a better position to contend with the more truculent left-wing elements in his party, including, of course, the *Jungsozialisten* who, as usual, were showing as much disappointment with the future as with the past. Then again, with the elections looming ever nearer it was important to show that even on this most contentious of issues the coalition partners – the Social Democrats on the one hand and the Free Democrats (representing in large measure the industrialists) on the other – were capable of harmonious co-operation at a time when there were rumours that this happy relationship was nearing its end. At all events, after some five years of interminable negotiation and heated argument, the Government suddenly brought forward a second bill, so skilfully drafted that it received a far greater degree of support – or, at least, absence of opposition – than those outside Government circles could possibly have foreseen.

The new bill in outline

It was not even an altogether new draft but was obviously based on the earlier bill the Government had submitted to the Bundestag in 1974 and which had never got beyond the Committee stage. It was indeed, a moot point whether that bill had been more disliked by employers or by unions; after coming under increasingly heavy fire it had finally foundered on the ingenious arguments, referred to earlier, that it was irreconcilable with the Federal Republic's 'Basic Law'. There were those in Government circles, however, who had been quietly taking note of all the major objections and, with consummate drafting skill, had been preparing a second version to

succeed where the first had failed. It was a legislative facelift carried out
by parliamentary draughtsmen with such dexterity as to remove warts and
blemishes without damaging the essential bone structure.

It may be that they were getting very tired by now or perhaps their
vision was growing dim, but in the eyes of the beholders the new bill began
to take on an attractiveness that had hitherto escaped their notice.
Possibly too, what happened is an illustration of the old saying that 'many
are stubborn in pursuit of the path they have chosen, few in pursuit of the
goal'. The bill now laid before them was certainly not the goal that some
of the protagonists had been pursuing (the DGB at least was in no doubt
about that) but for others it seemed to represent the end of the path they
had chosen. The realists saw that here was a chance at least to get
agreement on a piece of legislation that brought parity determination
nearer fulfilment while offering the enticing prospect of taking the issue out
of the election arena. The bill's scope is limited to companies with more
than 2000 employees (there are about 650 firms of this size) and covers the
following new ground:

At a first glance, workers appear at last to have been given parity with
shareholders (as in the coal and steel industries) on the Supervisory Board
(*Aufsichtsrat*). The bill ensures, however, that in the event of utter
deadlock – the 'Patt-Situation' that has been likened to a contest between
two scorpions in a corked bottle – it is the shareholders that will prevail.

This might not at first sight be apparent when looking at the
composition of the Supervisory Boards, which are made up equally of
shareholders and workers' representatives in the following proportions:

> Firms up to 10,000 employees   6:6
> Firms with from 10,000 to 20,000 employees   8:8
> Firms with over 20,000 employees   10:10

It is laid down, however, that on a Supervisory Board with ten workers'
representatives, seven are to be chosen from the shop floor and the staff of
the company and (this is the important point) one of them has to be a
leitender Angestellter. For the last two years and more, embittered
controversies have been raging over the role of the *leitender Angestellter*:
the term cannot be translated satisfactorily but perhaps the best definition
is that he is a salaried member of the staff whose duties include
responsibilities in which he has the final say – duties which have been
allotted to him on account of his skills and special experience. He is, in a
way, an 'executive' although it hardly seems quite correct to call him a
'senior executive' as is sometimes done. In any event, confusion is avoided
by sticking to the German term.

The rôle of this individual on a Supervisory Board is clearly vital. He is elected by his colleagues, i.e. other *leitende Angestellte*, without influence or pressure being exercised by the other groups. This, by the way, is precisely what the DGB and the Social Democrats had long sought to prevent. The unions had always hoped to ensure that the representative of the *leitende Angestellte* would be on their side, knowing full well that in the nature of things a *leitender Angestellter* tends to take the part of management, thus being an obstacle to the sort of 'parity' they wish to achieve. But this was a point on which the Free Democrats were prepared to fight to the last ditch; had they not in the end contrived to bring the Social Democrats around to their way of thinking the bill would never have re-appeared.

As for the other three 'workers' representatives' on a supervisory board employing over 20,000 employees, three must be union officials, i.e. persons not on the company's pay roll, although they all have to be elected by the work force. In firms with up to 8000 employees the election is done by direct secret ballot but in firms with more than 8000 employees the representatives are chosen by *Wahlmänner*, i.e. by a sort of electoral college.

In view of the appointment of the *leitender Angestellter* a stalemate or 'Patt-Situation' seems unlikely to arise but provision has been made for the chairman of the supervisory board to have a casting vote, to be put into effect when two polls have failed to achieve a majority decision.

The chairman of the Supervisory Board and the deputy-chairman require a two-thirds majority in order to get elected. If this two-thirds majority cannot be attained, the shareholders' representatives will make their nomination for chairman and the workers' representatives theirs for deputy-chairman. It should be added that the shareholders' representatives are elected at the Company's annual general meeting.

As regards the management board (*Vorstand*), which is responsible for the day-to-day running of the company, this is appointed by the Supervisory Board. A two-thirds majority is required but a complex process of mediation is provided for, at the end of which the chairman may use his casting vote. As in the coal and steel industries, one of the members of the management board must be a Labour Director (*Arbeitsdirektor*).

The coming into force of this new legislation means that there are now three separate forms of co-determination operating side by side in the Federal Republic, i.e.

(1) Parity Co-determination in the coal and steel industries in accordance with the Law of 1951, the *Mitbestimmungsgesetz*.

(2) One-third workers' representation in firms with less than 2000

employees, in accordance with the Works Constitution Law (*Betriebsverfassungsgesetz*) of 1971.

(3) The system described above, applicable to firms with more than 2000 employees (apart from the coal and steel industries). A two-year transitional period is envisaged, however, during which the re-alignment of the Supervisory Board (Aufsichtsrat) is being put into effect; the new Board would be expected to take up its functions after the second Annual General Meeting following the introduction of the new Law.

Although it is difficult at times to avoid the temptation of poking a little mild fun at some aspects of the co-determination controversy, there can be no doubt that, although the DGB's hopes have not been completely fulfilled, the Federal Republic has achieved and put into practice remarkably successful procedures for enabling workers to have a say in management. Without the untiring and devoted efforts of German trade unionists, able to hold their own in debate with politicians and academics of renown, this would never have been brought about.

Problems in applying the German solutions in Britain

It has to be recognised that there are many great difficulties, such as that of company law, that stand in the way of applying any of these three solutions to Britain – solutions which, in the last resort, despite all the theorising, have been worked out not on the campus but on German shop floors and board rooms and are backed by fifty years of practical experience. It should not be forgotten that during much of this time trade union representatives sitting on Supervisory Boards have been acquiring an ever-increasing and more intimate knowledge of, and insight into, the problems of management. Whatever the form of co-determination applied, it has done a great deal e.g. by works councils (and there seems no reason why these, at least, should not be established in Britain) to replace conflict and tension by co-operation and understanding. It is, in fact, difficult to over-estimate the significance of this German achievement in the modern industrial age; in many ways the Federal Republic's present economic prosperity and industrial peace is a demonstration of its success.

12

The part played by the Unions in the accumulation of assets by workers

The DGB and many of the unions have for years been active in furthering an interesting experiment known as *Vermögensbildung* – the accumulation of assets by workers. They have always been very conscious of the tendency for capital to be concentrated in the hands of the few, a trend which they hold to be counter to modern conceptions of economic and social order. This has been expressed in the words: 'Some people can become much better off more quickly, and without any appropriate effort on their part, than our social system intended'. A broader distribution of property would, the unions have urged, help both to ease tensions between capital and labour and to foster social harmony. Therefore they have from time to time brought pressure on the Government to speed up the process of helping the workers to build up their savings.

A sort of first faltering start might be said to have been made when workers were encouraged to acquire shareholdings in the Volkswagen undertaking; this was the occasion for grants and loans to be made generously available to help workers build their own homes. Private firms here and there had been trying out ingenious schemes of profit sharing but such schemes had little attraction for the unions and the first big step to meet their wishes was not made until 1961 when the Minister of Labour (Herr Blank, a Christian Democrat) steered through the Bundestag, with the strong support of the Socialist opposition, a law for the *Förderung der Vermögensbildung der Arbeitnehmer*. Incidentally, *Vermögensbildung* is wellnigh an impossible word to translate satisfactorily. Literally it means 'capital formation'. Perhaps 'promotion of personal assets' or 'promotion of personal savings' is as near as one can get.

The 1961 law

The 1961 law's high-sounding title (a law for the furtherance of property holding in the hands of workers) was rather belied by the modesty of its clauses but it broke new ground. It is usually referred to as the '312 DM Gesetz' as it freed employer and employee from the payment of social insurance contributions up to a limit of DM312 provided that an equivalent sum was set aside for savings purposes (*'Vermögenswirksame Leistung'*). It also freed an employee from the obligation of paying income tax on his earnings up to DM312 if his employer agreed to take over the commitment; the employer, in his turn, was then required to pay only 8% instead of the employee's full assessment (say about 20%) on the earnings in question. The aim was, of course, to ensure that, in addition to the cash payments which had hitherto been the basis of a worker's livelihood, he would receive additional emoluments to help him acquire property. The law also sought to encourage agreements between workers and employers for profit sharing (*Beteiligungen am Betriebsergebnis*).

The Leber plan

The trade unions were glad to see the law passed but they regarded it as falling far short of what they had a right to expect by way of a fairer re-distribution of income and only a few years elapsed before their discontent found expression in a positive programme for action enunciated in September 1964 by Georg Leber – later to become Minister of Transport (in December 1966) but still at that time head of the Construction Workers' Union. He elaborated suggestions for a new 'Employee Savings Plan', the gist of which was that employers should pay $1\frac{1}{2}$% of their outlay on wages into a reserve 'to be run similarly to an investment fund'.

This put the cat among the pigeons. The plan was immediately received with acclamation by a wide range of interests – newspapers, the catholic and evangelical churches and by the majority of unions. There was an ominous pause, however, before the employers – who, of course, were the most directly affected – discussed what line they had best take. Eventually they were at pains to emphasise how thoroughly sympathetic they were, in principle, to the conception that workers should acquire property and acquire it as quickly as possible; nevertheless they felt bound to express grave misgivings about the mechanics of the 'Leber Plan'. A scheme aimed at compulsory savings would, they suggested, contradict the very principle of freedom of choice – a principle valued not least by the workers themselves. Besides, German workers had been doing so well in recent years in accumulating property that there was really no need to adopt a plan to require them to do just this. The *Deutsches Industrie Institut* (an economic research institute run by employers and industrialists) produced a statement concerning the private accumulation of property in the Federal Republic in which, amid a profusion of statistics, figures were adduced to show that German workers had been acquiring savings and other forms of property to a degree and in a variety of ways unique in the history of mankind. For example, of some eighteen million households surveyed in 1962/63, 60% had savings accounts. Hundreds of thousands of building-loan accounts were being started every year and over two-thirds of the prospective new builders were wage-earners. Securities were possessed by two million holders. In short, workers were already acquiring property, why therefore put bounds on their freedom of action and compel them to save? No individual – least of all a worker – should, the employers argued, have his freedom circumscribed by obliging him to acquire property. The Free Democratic Party, as was to be expected from its close connection with industrialists, argued along similar lines.

No sooner had the *Industrie Institut's* views been ventilated than the Federal Ministry of Labour leapt into the fray, with counter arguments and a vastly different set of statistics to show that the workers were simply not saving enough; they were acquiring property infinitely more slowly than the self-employed. In a dispute of this kind in Germany each side inevitably invokes the aid of university professors. The DGB was delighted to see the Ministry of Labour basing much of its arguments on the researches of a certain Professor Föhl who sought to show that nearly 75% of the increase in private property in the ten years 1950 to 1959 had affected only 17% of households; it was the 'independents', not the workers, who were benefiting.

Matters now began to move quickly. The Cabinet decided to entrust the Federal Minister of Labour with the task of preparing a new Bill to try and speed up the process of getting property into the hands of the workers; the government was not only conscious of the proximity of the elections but envied the dexterity displayed by Herr Leber and the very considerable publicity which he was attracting as the great trade union advocate of the cause. Clearly fresh legislation would have to be prepared if the wind was to be taken out of his sails. It must in fairness be said, however, that the Christian Democrat Minister of Labour (himself a former very prominent trade unionist) had always consistently championed the cause of 'ownership for all in a free society' and was never weary of stressing that the 'proletariat of yesterday' would be remembered just so long as the workers were not themselves a property-owning class. 'Without property there can be no freedom' was a slogan he sought to make his own. He had realised at once that although Leber's formula related, strictly speaking, only to the building and civil engineering industries it obviously lent itself to much wider application; with remarkable celerity he came forward with the draft of a second *Vermögensbildungs-Gesetz* to amplify his earlier DM312 Law. This, despite the opposition of the Coalition partner, the Free Democrats, the Cabinet immediately accepted.

Improvements on the 1961 law

Compared with the earlier law the new enactment made the following improvements. Under the 1961 law an employee could only take advantage of its provisions if his employer agreed; he could then arrange for his wages (up to a maximum of DM312 in the year) to be set aside for savings purposes and was called upon to pay neither tax nor social insurance contributions in respect of that sum. The restrictions on the worker's access to the DM312 in his savings account were pretty lax. He could withdraw his savings at any time, the only 'penalty' for so doing being the loss of a 20% premium payable to those who left their money in their savings account for as long as 5½ years. While the 1961 law had laid it down that the special terms were only to be granted following direct agreement between worker and employer or on a basis of an individual works' agreement, the 1965 law expressly provided that its provisions could be the subject of collective agreements and that any worker could demand, as of right, that the savings concessions be applied in his case.

The 1965 law

Information is never easy to come by as to the practical effects of complicated legislation of this kind. During the height of the 1965 controversy, however, the Federal Ministry of Labour published the results of an enquiry it had been making into the extent to which the 1961 law had been used and even now, although so many years have since elapsed, the results may be of interest. The enquiry covered some 357,000 undertakings employing over twelve million workers, i.e. about two-thirds of the total number of employees in private industry, excluding agriculture and the distributive trades and other services. It was found that, while 2·1% of these undertakings had offered their employees the opportunity of adopting the DM312 savings procedure, only 1·2% had, in 1963, had their offer taken up (in 1961 the number had been only 0·5% and in 1962 0·8%). As to the extent to which workers had responded within those undertakings which offered them the benefits of the DM312 Law, only about one-tenth of the total eligible labour force had chosen to be covered (i.e. 2% of all the employees covered by the review); about 56% were white collar workers and 44% manual workers. On the average, the manual worker benefited up to the sum of DM249 and the white collar worker up to DM286. As regards the willingness of the firms to offer their workers the DM312 Law facilities, 2·1% of all undertakings, as already mentioned, responded. These firms employed, however, 20·3% of the labour force covered by the enquiry. In respect of 0·9% of the total number of undertakings surveyed there was no response from employees.

The discrepancy between the offer and the response seems to have taken the Minister aback. No good reason was found for this but it was suspected that in many cases the management's 'offer' might have been presented only in the form of a cursory enquiry of the works council or in some other inadequate and possibly off-hand manner. It did at least emerge pretty clearly that it was the larger undertakings that were most disposed to offer their workers the advantages of the scheme.

It was obvious, when a predominantly Socialist Coalition Government took office in October 1969, that it would lose little time in putting forward new proposals. At the end of February the new Minister of Labour – the former head of the Mine Workers' Union, Herr Arendt – presented an amending bill. On the face of it, his task was now less formidable than that which had confronted his predecessors. The employers had, in the last few years, wisely been changing their tune and, having been quite as badly frightened as the unions by the little display of shop-floor militancy in the 'wild week' of unofficial strikes in September 1969, they now saw great merits in proposals calculated to appeal to the more stable elements in the working community. They were conscious, too, that in the construction industry, famed for the happy relationships between the two sides, Leber's proposals for giving effect to *Vermögensbildung* by collective agreement had been a pronounced success. So Minister Arendt found almost everyone – with the significant exception of the Finance Ministers of the Länder – prepared in large measure to support him.

He put forward proposals which can be shortly summarised as follows:

(1) The DM312 Laws were now to be transformed into a DM624 Law – something that the Social Democrats and the unions had been urging for years. This meant, quite simply, doubling the amount of an employee's earnings that could be retained on his behalf for savings purposes from DM312 to DM624. It was the intention that this should be given retrospective effect from January 1970. Workers with three or more children were to be allowed to save up DM936 (instead of DM468, as hitherto).

(2) As from January 1971 the savings were to be liable to income tax and to social insurance contributions but they would attract a *Zulage* or bonus of 30%, which could either be credited or paid out of the worker. The intention of this *Zulage* was, of course, to help the lower paid workers; it had been alleged that the previous legislation favoured those in the higher income groups.

The 1970 bill
The bill went through the Bundestag with remarkably little trouble and

became law in the summer of 1970. The Minister's remarks at the time of the passing of the law summarised pretty accurately the views of his trade union colleagues. He regarded it as making possible the ultimate success of 'Vermögensbildung'; more collective agreements with really adequate conditions and arrangements could in future be drawn up between the two sides of industry. He said that in anticipation of the passing of the law many agreements had already come into force during the last few months covering about twelve million workers, i.e. half the total number of the employed labour force. After referring to the doubling of the scope of benefits with retrospective effect from 1 January 1970, he repeated his earlier pledge that further adaptations of the existing laws on *Vermögensbildung* would take effect to ensure that savings made in accordance with the provisions laid down would no longer be free from tax and social insurance payments. Instead, the State would pay premiums on the savings amounting in general to 30% but in the case of families with three or more children 40%; income limits would be introduced of DM24,000 for single persons and DM48,000 for married couples. Incidentally, a corresponding law extended the same *Vermögenswirksame Leistungen* as those granted in January 1970 to workers and salaried staffs of the public services, to judges, civil servants, professional soldiers and men doing their military service.

The unions, even those that had shown least enthusiasm about *Vermögensbildung*, immediately set about adding greatly to the number and scope of the relevant collective agreements so as to take advantage of the possibilities now presented. Even the Metal Workers' Union, that had constantly expressed misgivings, achieved a real break-through by concluding an agreement with the Engineering Employers Confederation (*Gesamtmetall*) providing for four million workers to get a sort of income-tax-free dividend of DM26 a month as from 1 July 1970. This sum may at first sight seem insignificant but it has to be recalled that, taking the interest and bonuses granted from the Treasury for long-term savings into account, those concerned were able to accumulate a sum of DM3360 in $5\frac{1}{2}$ years; this involved industry in a charge of some DM8,000,000,000.

It is hardly necessary to point to the social significance of the scheme. It clearly gives the workers a stake in the success of Germany's social and economic system. A remarkable feature of the last few years has been the changed attitude to it of employers and employers' associations; those who were once unenthusiastic if not actually hostile have since shown willingness to meet the unions half-way in drawing up collective agreements to comply with the terms of the law. It is not easy to assess the scope of its coverage but a survey undertaken by the DGB's Economic Research Institute (WSI) in 1974 showed that thirteen million workers were already covered in 1973 by collective agreements giving them DM312 yearly in addition to their wages or salary, the employers concerned having undertaken to find DM4 milliards for the purpose. The scheme is now believed to cover some eighteen million workers.

The DM624 Law still holds the field but at one stage it looked as if the present Parliament might approve a still more far-reaching supplementary scheme. In January 1974, just as the Coalition Government was putting forward its original controversial proposals for new legislation on *Mitbestimmung*, it simultaneously announced some startling new proposals on *Vermögensbildung*. Reference has already been made to the intense controversy to which the *Mitbestimmung* proposals gave rise, resulting in their abandonment but eventual successful resuscitation after skilful redrafting. A very different fate awaited the *Vermögensbildung* proposals. These, by contrast, were quietly and not unfavourably received at the outset, only to encounter later on such increasingly persistent and dogged opposition that the Government thought it best to let the issue quietly drop.

As the Government's proposals never came to anything it is necessary to say very little about them. The aim was to spread ownership of capital by procuring it through a graduated levy on all firms whose annual profits after operating taxes (*Betriebssteuern*) exceeded DM400,000. Oddly enough, it was the opposition of some of the unions that played a considerable part in getting the proposals defeated. The head of the Metal Workers Union, Eugen Loderer, and the leaders of some other large unions opposed them on grounds that planned saving or 'pretty shareholding' is no substitute for 'money in hand'. Their objections had, of course, nothing in common with those of a small radical left-wing element which considered that to encourage participation in profit sharing is to blunt the opposition of the workers to the capitalist system by involving them directly in it. Probably the average savings-conscious German worker would have been not ill-pleased had the proposals gone through; an average yield from firms of DM5000 million in the first year would have given some 23 million beneficiaries a yearly sum of about DM212.

But yet another factor that led to the proposals being dropped was the truly formidable array of technical and legal problems involved. These would have necessitated the setting up of interdepartmental working groups with experts from the four or five Government departments concerned. At least fifty acts of Parliament would have required amendment and the new scheme could not have been brought into operation before January 1978 at the earliest. It is hardly surprising that the Government thought it best to let *Vermögensbildung* pursue its quiet and unspectacular way under the well-tried provisions of the DM624 Law, leaving it to the opposition, the CDU/CSU, to point with such enthusiasm as it could muster to the many and varied profit-sharing schemes, based on a dozen or so 'participation' models, that some two hundred individual companies have been operating for many years and which now seem to be finding their way back into the limelight.

13

The present state and aims of German Trade Unionism

What is to be said of the present state of German trade unionism? Its 'golden age', characterised by constant increases in standards of living, relative freedom from industrial strife and a minimum of friction and dissension, seems to be over. Trade union leaders have to be increasingly on their guard these days against the activities of small well-organised groups – Maoists, Trotskyists and other *Radikalinskis* loosely organised in the 'Revolutionary Trade Union Opposition' (*Revolutionäre Gewerkschaftsopposition* or RGO) that are much less concerned with the real interests of trade unionists than in stirring up militancy and discord with the ultimate aim of establishing a 'dictatorship of the proletariat'. Some unions have amended their constitutions to guard against this danger and – fortunately for the Federal Republic's economy – German trade union leadership seems to be combating these activities with the same energy as was displayed in the hectic days of the late 'forties when Böckler and his colleagues put the Ruhr Communists to rout. Supported by the overwhelming majority of trade unionists, the movement they built up has remained remarkably free from fanatical ideology, misconception and prejudice. Most of the older leaders have now been replaced by much younger men but these, like their predecessors, are among the most able and conscientious men in German public life. Their task has certainly become more difficult in recent years in that orthodox, easily identifiable Communists were less of a danger to union leadership than the exponents of new brands of Marxism who conduct their activities with a skilful eye to cover. It is only at trade union congresses in the last few years that they have sometimes been forced to come into the open – thereby, at least, much enlivening the proceedings!

The political attitudes

Some observers see another danger to the best interests of German trade unionism in its increasing tendency to become a little too closely involved in the political scene. The conviction that a trade union movement must be independent of Government and of political parties is widely held in the Federal Republic. The principal lessons of the 'thirties have not been forgotten and German trade unionists accept neither the principle observed in Communist countries that the primary purpose of trade unions is to serve the State, nor have they been led into the contrary error of regarding themselves as exclusively concerned with workers' interests, heedless of whatever harm may thereby be done to the State and the nation's economy. But while the German trade union movement is *überparteilich*, Vetter has stressed time and again that this is far from meaning that it is politically neutral. In the nature of things it tends to be more in sympathy with the aims of a Social-Democratic (SPD) Government than with those of the Conservative Christian-Democrats. Vetter is held in some quarters to have gone a little too far in emphasising his preference for the Social-Democratic Party (SPD) and some have complained that he has been more forthright in his championship of Social-Democratic aims than his predecessors. It must be remembered, however, that the SPD was not in power in the days when they held office.

A change of attitude to political matters within a few unions was discernible after the success of the Social-Democrats at the 1969 election. This, naturally enough, delighted trade union members of the Party but led for the first time to noticeable tensions between Social Democratic and Christian Democratic trade unionists – tensions which, if they existed, had previously seldom come to the surface. It seemed ominous when a very able member of the Executive Committee of one of the larger unions failed to get re-elected in September 1972 for no other apparent reason than that he was a member of the Christian-Democratic Party; just about the same time the Köln District Committee of the Union of Workers in Public Services, Transport and Communications (ÖTV) went so far as to threaten its most prominent member, Herr Katzer, the previous CDU Minister of Labour, with expulsion for having commented on SPD preferences within the union. Such discords, including those between moderate and left-of-centre Social Democratic trade unionists, naturally provide opportunities for mischief which left-wing extremists are not slow to exploit – extremists who range from honest idealists, often closely associated with the *Jung Sozialisten*, to the downright fanatics of the *Revolutionär-Kommunistische Jugend*. (Bomb-planting revolutionaries have not chosen to interest themselves in German trade union affairs.) The two incidents referred to served at least the useful purpose of making it clear to most thoughtful trade unionists that the movement can ill afford divisions between its Socialist and 'Christian' elements; they are well aware that the worst thing that could happen would be the formation of a break-away Christian Trade Union movement – a danger that still seems as remote as ever. The DGB remains true to its tradition of having two Christian-Democrats (Maria Weber and Martin Heiss) on its Federal Executive Committee.

Although – largely owing to the statemanship and restraint of the unions over so many years – the Federal Republic has a lower rate of inflation (5·3%) than anywhere else in western Europe, the rate is high enough to give concern to many Germans who, having regard to their country's unfortunate experience in the nineteen-twenties, are aware that unemployment is an inevitable consequence of inflation. Fear of unemployment is a factor that the Government has had constantly to reckon with in recent years, but it has been assured of the support of the unions in any reasonable steps it may find necessary to take.

Re-examination of aims and achievements

Without going over ground already covered in previous chapters this is perhaps the place to mention that, although the German trade union movement cannot for a moment be accused of ideological fanaticism, its preoccupation with *paritätische Mitbestimmung* is inevitably regarded in some quarters as excessive; the movement would hardly be characteristically German, however, if it did not attempt to define its aims and objectives with painstaking exactitude and a touch of philosophic fervour. Whatever one's views on this controversial topic may be, it is unlikely, even after the passing of the 1976 Co-determination Law, that the leadership will draw back from urging a unique conception of co-partnership to which it has devoted an enormous amount of time and energy. That no other western European country could attempt to put such a system into operation does not necessarily mean that it cannot be made to work in the Federal Republic.

A great deal of thinking and re-thinking is in fact always going on within DGB headquarters at Düsseldorf: the movement believes that it must constantly re-examine its aims and not rest content with achievements that would have been thought impossible of attainment in the early 'fifties. A statement put out some years ago by the Federal Ministry of Labour still succinctly summarises the position: 'Western Germany enjoys the highest wages, the shortest working hours, the most frequent holidays, and the longest leave of all European countries'. The trade union movement looks back with understandable pride to a time when the unions were acknowledged champions of the democratic way of life – a time, indeed, when sceptics were doubting whether democracy could ever take root in German soil.

The unions have never lost sight of the link between individual

endeavour, or lack of it, and material wealth. Claims for wage increases have consistently been kept within the limits of what industry could afford, despite allegations from employers to the contrary; many feared that the unions might not hold back, as they did in 1974 and in 1975 and are doing yet again in 1976. At the turn of the year, 250,000 steelworkers settled for a 5% wage increase, a display of moderation that once again set the pattern. The headquarters of the union concerned, I.G. Metall, issued a statement to the effect that its members were 'more interested in keeping their jobs than enlarging their pay packets'. It is hardly surprising that the unions' moderation and responsibility have been so often praised not only by the present Federal Chancellor but by his predecessors. The success of the unions in convincing most of their membership of the simple but elusive fact that it is higher industrial production that creates the wealth that makes the payment of higher wages possible, explains why there has been such an enormous improvement in the standards of living of the working population. Inflation, small though it is in comparison with other countries, has in the last two or three years been making matters more difficult, but the fact remains that from 1962 to 1972 wages rose by as much as 120·9% while the cost of living went up by only 39·6% – and all the time Western Germany's economic and financial prosperity has continued to be the envy of her neighbours.

The unions' spirit of self criticism

Although the DGB is proud of its achievements and does not hesitate to draw attention to them, a marked characteristic of the labour organisations in the Federal Republic is that they are permeated by a healthy spirit of self criticism. There is a ready disposition to examine and re-examine any system that shows itself unequal to meeting the problems presented by the unprecedented industrial and technological developments that characterise the modern age. This applies, by the way, as much to management as it does to the unions.

A survey of managerial practice carried out a few years back ended with the statement: 'There is no such thing as scientific management. There is good management and there is bad management; the difference between the two is mainly one of complacency.' Complacency is the last thing anyone has even associated with German management or with the unions; it is significant, moreover, that the management of the great majority of German undertakings have long recognised the need to spend at least as much care on the development of their work-people as on the development of their machines. The unions, naturally jealous of their prerogatives, sometimes tend to be suspicious of this attitude on the part of management. They are no doubt justified in ridiculing it when it appears in the exaggerated form of paternalism but there can be no doubt that it has often smoothed the way for the exercise of their own legitimate functions.

The wage structure

The wage structure of West Germany might commend itself as worthy of study. The German trade union movement has always tried to ensure that the lowest paid workers earn an adequate wage; the aim has been to maintain a reasonably well-balanced wage scale avoiding undue disparities between industries. The DGB's Wages Policy Department is always active behind the scenes in co-ordinating trade union wages policy with the aim of maintaining a reasonably well-balanced wage scale avoiding such disparities of this kind; the result has been that although adequate differentials (and thereby, incentives) have been maintained, even unskilled workers at the bottom of the wage scale, e.g. in the shoe and leather processing industries, are able to maintain a good standard of living. The system of establishing an *Ecklohn* from which percentage wage increases are calculated helps to ensure that all workers benefit proportionately from wage increases while reasonable differentials are not ignored; the growing weight attached to a *Sockelbetrag* or 'base sum' is also significant.

The success the German unions have had in helping to stimulate productivity while keeping within bounds the tendency for workers in certain favoured industries to do disproportionately better than their less fortunate colleagues in other industries is shown by the fact that, a few years back, before recent inflationary trends made themselves evident, the average weekly wage of an unskilled worker was already DM290 (say £48); the average for all grades over all industries was DM340 (say £57). Since then the most recent wage statistics available (for 1974) show that male industrial workers were paid on the average DM9.68 an hour and women DM6.90 an hour; the highest earnings were, not surprisingly, in the oil and printing industries. In the least well-paid industries hourly pay rates averaged just over DM8. The absence of excessive discrepancies in the wages of the highest and lowest paid workers shows that the 'get all you can when you can' stance is no more favoured by German than by Austrian unions.

The 'working classes' – to use a phrase somewhat out of place now that the last traces of a cloth-cap proletariat are vanishing from the German scene – have been improving their position, economically and, perhaps even more important, culturally, to the point at which they are almost indistinguishable from the so-called 'middle classes'. The *Ruhrfestspiele* (Ruhr Festival) at Recklinghausen is only one example of what the trade

union movement is doing to encourage arts and the theatre. The Ruhr
Festival, indeed, is tending more and more to become a 'Cultural Month
of Trade Unionism'.

The 1963 Programme of Action announced that the movement is
'permeated with a sense of responsibility to its membership and the whole
German people; ... the challenge of the twentieth century has been
accepted'. Such phraseology may appear to some to be flamboyant but
there is no doubting its utter sincerity. Slogans about workers 'lying
prostrate at the mercy of a rapacious capitalist economy' have been shown
by the movement to be utterly ridiculous. Everyone knows that the
German trade union movement has itself become in many ways one of the
most successful capitalist undertakings within the federal Republic; it is
only necessary to mention the trade unions' *Bank für Gemeinwirtschaft* or
Neue Heimat in this connection. But the point is that it has all been to the
advantage of the workers. The familiar words of the American trade
unionist, Dubinsky, that 'trade unions need capitalism just as much as a
fish needs water' assume a fresh significance where West Germany is
concerned.

The association with capitalism

This association with capitalism – an association that helps to explain the
dislike felt for German trade unionism in certain quarters – is not entirely
welcome to the DGB's own thinkers. By accepting capitalism and the free
market economy the German trade union movement has become one of
the most outstandingly successful in the free world; so far, so good. But it
is urged that the next task is to get the capitalist system re-shaped and
modified in the interests of the whole community. A new 'Programme of
Action' drawn up by the DGB at its triennial Congress in Berlin in 1972
threw much light on its forward aims. It marked another stage forward
from the 1963 'Programme of Action' – adopted at an Extraordinary
Congress in Düsseldorf – that was mainly notable for throwing overboard
a good deal of the ideological ballast that still survived from the bad old
days of class warfare; on the whole, despite an occasional spatchcock, the
document was a level-headed statement of legitimate trade union desires
and objectives at that time. But the 1972 document defined those desires
and objectives afresh, with particular reference to the position of the
unions in a capitalist state. It is, in essence, a confident assertion of trade
union determination never to rest until the benefits conferred by almost
uninterrupted industrial peace, increasing rationalisation and productivity
are more fairly distributed to the populace as a whole. 'Socialism by
gradual evolution', in fact.

Major aims and objectives

The 1972 programme's major aims and objective may be briefly summarised as follows: shorter working hours, longer annual holidays, implementation of the 8-hour five day week throughout the economy, higher wages and salaries (e.g. a larger share of the proceeds of the economy for the workers, equal pay for equal work, fringe benefits written into collective agreements if not otherwise guaranteed by legislation), a more equitable distribution of wealth, improved taxation and fiscal policy (e.g. a redistribution of the overall burden of taxation to the benefit of the lower-income brackets), job security (security of full employment by means of a forward-looking governmental labour market policy, adequate measures to avert the adverse consequences of rationalisation and automation, a programme for the protection of older workers against the social consequences of economic and technical change), improved social security, improved provisions for retirement (e.g. every worker to be given the option of retiring at the age of sixty, retirement pensions assessed at 75% of final earnings, separate and independent pensions entitlement for women), the codification of Labour Law and the abolition of social and labour legislation divergencies between manual and non-manual workers, a re-definition of the legal status of established officials in the public service, more co-determination (e.g., a requirement on the part of multi-national undertakings in the EEC to establish Supervisory Boards on which both sides of industry are equally represented), equality of educational chances and improved vocational training (*inter alia*, ten years' full-time compulsory schooling in all *Länder*, the introduction of integrated comprehensive schools, public control of vocational education, greater finance allocations for re-training, and additional paid time-off for educational purposes), improvement of the law on rent contracts and building land (e.g. improved promotion of social house building for the benefit of low-income groups and improvements of the law on the protection of tenants) and more effective protection against environmental pollution.

This ambitious programme, spelt out in such detail at the 1972 Congress, will obviously require many years to achieve. Meanwhile, the DGB has left it in no doubt that it is intent on obtaining for the trade union movement a further increase in power and authority – accepting without hesitation the additional responsibility this would bring with it. The confidence which the movement now reposes in Herr Vetter and its wish to remain on the course he has set for it was clearly indicated at the Congress held in Hamburg in 1975. He was re-elected by an even more impressive majority than he had been three years earlier at Berlin, now getting as many as 440 votes out of a possible 450. When first elected in succession

to Ludwig Rosenberg at the 1969 Munich Congress he had won only 267
votes, and there had been as many as 133 abstentions, but at that time he
was not widely known except as an efficient Deputy President of the Mine
Workers' Union. He has since become accepted everywhere as the
movement's philosopher and spokesman and if at times the forthright
clarity of his language has drawn down upon him an accusation of 'Verbal-
Radikalismus'—this is the sort of criticism from which no prominent
personality in public life can for long be immune.

No review of German trade unionism would be complete that did not
refer to the vast extent of its international activities. It is doubtful, indeed,
whether any trade union movement is quite so internationally-minded as
the German—not forgetting the overseas activities of the AFL/CIO. No
sooner had the movement re-established itself than it began to play an
increasingly important role in the International Confederation of Free
Trade Unions (ICFTU) and the leaders of some of the principal unions soon
began to be elected to presidential posts on various International Trade
Secretariats (it is only necessary to recall the names of Gefeller, Brenner,
Gutermuth, Stenger and Buschmann in this connection). Willi Richter,
who became President of the DGB in October 1956 (being made at about
the same time Vice-President of the ICFTU) set a pattern for his successors,
Rosenberg and Vetter, to follow. He was a member of the ILO's Governing
Body at Geneva and played a conspicuous part at an important moment
in aiding trade unionism in the developing countries.

But it was left for the DGB's Hamburg Congress of 1975 to come out
with greater emphasis than ever before on the rôle of trade unionism in
international affairs. It seems best to let Herr Vetter be his own
mouthpiece by quoting from the important address he gave on that
occasion:

'Economic, political and social challenges in the next few years will
stretch to the utmost the mental and material potential of the trade
unions. We must give convincing answers to new questions and I have
no doubt that we will. If we don't, we shall lose the confidence of the
workers and trade union influence on politicians and on the economy
will melt away.

'We must fight injustice with good sense, sympathy and the courage
to be truthful. We must be just as much on guard against resignation
and fatalism as against cynics and fanatics. It is the only way we can
remain credible and the only way we can preserve our ability to
activate others for trade union aims. . . .

The main challenge facing us is the widening disparity between rapid
technological progress and people's limited capability meaningfully to
put that progress to use. . . . All this computerized progress has been

incapable of driving hunger from the world. . . .

Difficulties in our own country must not prevent us from realising that every national policy is interwoven with a whole network of international relations and responsibilities. Trade union policy cannot be national village pump policy either. The Federal Republic of Germany is the strongest economic power in Europe. In exports we rank immediately after the USA, with Japan quite a long way off in third place, followed by France and Britain. Such economic power puts us under obligation. . . .

Worldwide economic and social structures have a decisive bearing on the national economy. In view of the fact that every fifth job in the Federal Republic depends on exports, this connection should not surprise anyone. Isolationism and self-sufficiency are pacemakers of a new world economic crisis. It is therefore in the trade interests of all for the developing countries to become viable partners in international trade. . . .

The world is knocking harder and more doggedly on our door. And that means that we must invest more thought, more time and more money than hitherto in our international commitments.'

The DGB's activities to which Herr Vetter refers are not, of course, invariably looked upon with favour by all sections of international trade unionism. On the one hand, left-wing elements of European trade unions regard the German movement as dangerously 'pro-capitalist'; on the other, it has been condemned as 'too friendly to Communism' by the American trade union movement (AFL/CIO). Vetter had occasion in the course of his speech to make the remark; 'Particularly distressing for the unity of the free trade union world is our failure so far to bring the American trade union federation, AFL/CIO, back into the International Confederation of Free Trade Unions.' The frank exchange of correspondence on this issue some two or three years back, between Mr. George Meany, President of the AFL/CIO and Vetter is still relevant. In the course of this Vetter defended the DGB's attitude at length and it seems appropriate to conclude by stating his position once more in his own words by quotations from the letter he wrote on 17th August 1973 (given in its English version in the DGB Report of December 1973), as follows:

'Germany and with it the Federal Republic is a country of the centre, at least for Europe. Its integration in the 'United States of Europe', desired and striven for with every effort by us, by no means leads us as a people and society out of the frontier situation to the states and peoples of Eastern Europe. This inevitable closeness to the social systems prevailing there obliges us, whether we want to or not, to deal actively and intellectually with the people and the ideas of the Soviet Union and its allies. . . . If the political leaders of the Federal Republic after two world wars which began in Europe have viewed their historical task as upholding the peace for the whole of Europe, then they could always be certain of the active support of the trade unions, which have indeed made détente and peace the main aim of their statutes. . . . Scarcely a trade union movement in the world has had to experience more fervently than the German that all trade union activity is superfluous if peace is not also established and maintained internationally. Two spheres of activity result for us from this. In the first place in the West, to create the United States of Europe with the assistance of our brother organisations and their political force. We are still on the way, but I am convinced that the egoism of certain members of the European Communities which emerges time and again cannot stand in the way of the Federal state in Western Europe. Economic co-operation has developed so far that as early as 1969 we were able to juxtapose this West European economy with an appropriate trade union organisation – the European Union of Free Trade Unions.' (Now the European Trade Union Confederation (ETUC)). '. . . The trade unions are obliged more than any other group of German society to work for permanent détente and a lasting peace, here lies the essential reason for our contacts with the East.'

And as regards the European Trade Union Confederation, at the Congress at which he was unanimously elected president (in succession to Lord Feather) Vetter summarised the aims of that Confederation in the words 'that we all work together to shape this young organisation into a determined, active instrument for Europe's workers'.

Appendix I

Principal Trade Unions in the Federal Republic of Germany

The German Trade Union Federation

	Dec. 1973	Dec. 1974	Dec. 1975
1. The Industrial Union of Workers in Building, Quarrying and Public Works Contracting, Frankfurt (*IG Bau, Steine, Erden*)			
Total Membership	522,157	517,902	509,422
2. The Industrial Union of Workers in Mines and Energy, Bochum (*IG Bergbau und Energie*)			
Total Membership	377,589	374,082	378,369
3. The Industrial Union of Chemical, Paper and Pottery Workers, Hannover (*IG Chemie, Papier, Keramik*)			
Total Membership	645,178	655,703	644,271
4. The Industrial Union of Printing and Paper Processing Workers, Stuttgart (*IG Druck und Papier*)			
Total Membership	160,062	164,465	157,985
5. The Union of German Railwaymen, Frankfurt (*Gewerkshaft der Eisenbahner Deutschlands*)			
Total Membership	444,229	455,380	447,914
6. The Union of Educational and Scientific Workers, Frankfurt (*Gewerkschaft Erziehung und Wissenschaft*)			
Total Membership	132,430	132,106	139,294
7. The Union of Horticultural, Agricultural and Forestry Workers, Kassel-Wilhelmshöhe (*Gewerkschaft Gartenbau, Land- und Forstwirtschaft*)			
Total Membership	40,009	39,859	39,309
8. The Union of Salaried Employees in Trade and Commerce, Banks and Insurance, Düsseldorf (*Gewerkschaft Handel, Banken und Versicherungen*)			
Total Membership	210,038	236,642	257,123
9. The Union of Wood and Plastic Workers, Düsseldorf (*Gewerkschaft Holz und Kunststoff*)			
Total Membership	134,817	135,205	132,054

104   TRADE UNIONS IN WEST GERMANY

	Dec. 1973	Dec. 1974	Dec. 1975
10. The Union of Artists (including Stage, Variety, Film, Radio, Musicians, Commercial Artists, etc.), Düsseldorf (*Gewerkschaft Kunst*) *Total Membership*	35,618	36,150	36,461
11. The Union of Leather Workers, Stuttgart (*Gewerkschaft Leder*) *Total Membership*	58,860	57,600	56,458
12. The Industrial Union of Metal Workers, Frankfurt (*IG Metall*) *Total Membership*	2,460,697	2,593,480	2,556,184
13. The Union of Food, Drink, Tobacco and Catering Trade Workers, Hamburg (*Gewerkschaft Nahrung, Genuss, Gaststätten*) *Total Membership*	251,879	248,481	248,724
14. The Union of Workers in Public Services, Transport and Communications, Stuttgart (*Gewerkschaft Öffentliche Dienste, Transport und Verkehr*) *Total Membership*	997,771	1,051,098	1,058,525
15. The German Postal Workers Union, Frankfurt (*Deutsche Postgewerkschaft*) *Total Membership*	400,624	419,966	419,585
16. The Union of Textile and Clothing Workers, Düsseldorf (*Gewerkschaft Textil-Bekleidung*) *Total Membership*	295,565	287,641	283,234
GRAND TOTAL OF D.G.B. UNIONS	7,167,523*	7,405,760†	7,364,912‡

German Salaried Employees Union (*Deutsche Angestellten-Gewerkschaft* – or DAG), Hamburg
Total Membership Approx. 475,000

The Union of Civil Servants and Officials (*Deutscher Beamtenbund* – or DBB) *Bad Godesberg*
Total Membership Approx. 650,000 (including retired members)

*Including 1,180,000 women; †including 1,284,500 women; ‡including 1,313,021 women

Appendix II

'Strike Law' is a convenient, if somewhat inaccurate, way of referring to the various rules and regulations which govern industrial disputes in West Germany. A useful legislative foundation has been provided but many of the rules have been written into the constitutions of the various trade unions in close conformity with the recommendations of the Trade Union Confederation's Munich Congress of 1949. Something like a case-law has been built up by decisions of the Labour Courts (*Arbeitsgerichte*), particularly as regards *Arbeitskampfrecht*.

Collective Agreements Law

The major piece of legislation governing labour disputes is the *Tarifvertragsgesetz* (Collective Agreements Law). This defines precisely what is meant by a collective agreement, specifies the persons and organisations entitled to enter into such agreements and indicates their scope. The law does not, however, attempt to deal with the situation that arises once wage negotiations have finally broken down, i.e. when the two parties pass from the state of peace (*Frieden*) obtaining during the currency of the collective agreement to the industrial warfare (*Krieg*) that may arise on its termination. The law provides that either party to a collective agreement has the right, once the specified period of validity of a collective agreement expires, to give formal notice (*kündigen*) that the agreement is terminated. Any breach of contract by either side during the validity of the agreement is liable to heavy penalties but once the agreement is terminated the parties are free to take their negotiations to the point of commencing actual industrial warfare (strike or lock-out as the case may be) provided all the possibilities of reaching a settlement have first been exhausted.

Conciliation

In most industries the two sides have drawn up elaborate procedures for conciliation which have to be gone through before a strike or lock-out can be declared. As a general rule, the conciliation procedures work well and the unfortunate difficulties that arose during the Metal Workers' strike (set out in some detail in Chapter 6) should not be regarded as typical. Conciliation normally takes place at the regional (Land or *Bezirk*) level and a typical arrangement is for conciliation committees to be comprised at Land level of two representatives of employers and union respectively; if conciliation fails at Land level (*Landesschlichtung*) the matter goes up to a national conciliation committee (*Bundesschlichtung*), at which each side has three representatives. Once the conciliation procedures have been exhausted the obligation on the two sides to maintain industrial peace (*Friedenspflicht*) is removed.

Secret Ballot Procedures (Urabstimmung)

The Chemical Workers' Union is the only one of the sixteen DGB unions which does not expressly require a secret ballot of the membership concerned to be taken before strike action can begin. It was at its 1963 Congress in Wiesbaden that the union amended its constitution so as to empower its central executive to take strike action without necessarily first taking a secret ballot – a decision which caused much controversy.

Strikes

A strike is regarded as a last resort to be adopted only after all other procedures have been exhausted. It by no means follows that strike action, once taken, is going to affect any large part of an industry either nationally or at Land level (i.e. a *Vollstreik*). The unions usually prefer to organise warning strikes so as to test the feelings of their membership while watching the effect on public opinion. Picketing is, of course, legal provided there is no physical interference with 'strike-breakers', who may only be 'spoken to' by the pickets. It has sometimes been known for such discussions to end in blows, e.g. during the Chemical Workers' dispute, almost invariably due to provocation offered by extremists anxious to take full advantage of the opportunities picketing affords them and whose humourless truculence makes them markedly unreceptive to friendly banter. (A short summary of the law on 'picketing' has been added to this Appendix.)

Streikgeld (Strike Pay)

Strikers are entirely dependent for the duration of the strike on the money provided by their union. (The State remains scrupulously neutral and makes no payment either to the striker or to his family.) The amount of strike money varies from one union to another but the amounts paid by the Chemical Workers' Union (set out in Chapter 7) can be taken as fairly typical.

Emergency Service (Notdienst)

For the duration of a strike an emergency service is always carried out by selected workers to ensure that the plant remains in good order so as to enable productive processes to be resumed the moment the dispute ends.

THE LAW IN REGARD TO 'PICKETING' IN WEST GERMANY

Picketing (*Das Streikpostenstehen*) is in principle not illegal in the Federal Republic so long as the pickets use only peaceful persuasion (*solange die Posten nur gütlich auf die Arbeitswilligen einwirken*). It is an offence to use force, e.g. to threaten non-striking employees, to assault them or to prevent them by forceful means from entering the place of work where the strike is taking place or by any other means to exercise constraint upon them. If the strike leaders tolerate such illegal acts by the pickets or even go so far as to sponsor them, the strike itself may become illegal. If, however, such infringements by pickets are committed against the wishes of the strike leaders, the legality of the dispute itself is not thereby affected but the pickets themselves become personally liable for the injuries they inflict upon the non-strikers and make themselves liable to be charged for obstruction, insult, bodily harm, and deprivation of liberty, as well as for breach of the peace. They cannot plead in justification of their action that it was undertaken in their capacity as pickets in an industrial dispute; neither may the pickets prevent the delivery or dispatch of raw materials and goods.

Bibliography

Much of the limited material available in English on the subject of German trade unionism is in the form of short summaries.

A brief account is given in Franz Lepinski's *German Trade Union Movement* (a translation of his *Die Gewerkschaftsbewegung in Deutschland*) published by the DGB. A more recent DGB publication is Dieter Schuster's *The German Labour Movement*.

Alfred Grosser's *Western Germany: From Defeat to Rearmament* (translated from the French and published by George Allen and Unwin Ltd. in 1955) has a good deal to say about the background against which the German trade union movement was re-created.

As regards works in German, *Politik und Programmatik des Deutschen Gewerkschaftsbundes* by Gerhard Leminsky and Bernd Otto (*Bund-Verlag, Köln*) contains a wealth of detailed information while Dr. Bernd Otto's *Gewerkschaftliche Konzeptionen überbetrieblicher Mitbestimmung* contains a very useful bibliography which refers not only to the more important works on 'Mitbestimmung' but also to many dealing with other aspects of German trade unionism. In *Zwischenbilanz der Mitbestimmung* by Potthoff, Blume and Duvernell (*Tübingen, 1962*) Dr. Potthoff traces the historical development of *Mitbestimmung* in the coal and steel industries.

The *Betriebsverfassungsgesetz* of 1971 has been translated by the International Labour Office (Legislative Series 1972 – Ger. F.R.1) and reprinted both by the Federal Ministry of Labour in Bonn and by the Bundesvereinigung der Deutschen Arbeitgeberverbände in Köln.

If a copy can still be obtained, *Die Gewerkschaftsbewegung in der britischen Besatzungszone* (published by the Bund-Verlag, Köln, in 1949) gives an invaluable account of the revival of German trade unionism in the crucial years 1947/9.

Those interested in the development of the Deutsche Angestellten-Gewerkschaft and the Deutscher Beamtenbund may wish to approach the headquarters of those organisations in Hamburg and in Bonn/Bad

Godesberg respectively. Well illustrated accounts are available, e.g. *Die Deutsche Angestellten-Gewerkschaft* (Buchreihe Mensch und Gesellschaft) and *Deutscher Beamtenbund – Werden und Wirken* (Walhalla und Praetoria Verlag, Regensburg).

In general, those wishing to keep in touch with the day-to-day activities of German trade unions may wish to refer to such periodicals as the DGB's *Welt der Arbeit* and those of the individual unions, e.g. the Metal Workers' Union's *Monatsschrift 'Der Gewerkschafter'*. The German Embassy also issues from time to time helpful informatory pamphlets (in English) on such matters as *Mitbestimmung* and *Vermögensbildung*.

Index